Retire Well with Less Money

**Retire Happily and Live the Life of Your Dreams
An Ultimate Guide**

Steven Young

I dedicate this book to every American out there who wants to change their concept about retiring and knowing that anything is possible and how to have a fulfilled life after all the hard work and dedications in your career. As sure as you it can get you to a more satisfying life and full of memories when you retired. Isn't it a music in your ear when you retire happy, satisfied and will live a bountiful, fulfilling life.

Copyright Act of 1976, the scanning, uploading and electronic sharing of any part of this book without the explicit written consent or permission of the publisher constitutes unlawful piracy and the theft of intellectual property.

If you would like to use material or content from this book (other than for review purposes), prior written permission must be obtained from the publisher.

You can contact the publishing company at admin@speedypublishing.com. Thank you for not infringing on the author's rights.

Speedy Publishing LLC (c) 2014
40 E. Main St., #1156
Newark, DE 19711
www.speedypublishing.co

Ordering Information:
Quantity sales; Special discounts are available on quantity purchases by corporations, associations, and others. For details, contact the "Special Sales Department" at the address above.

This is a reprint book.

Manufactured in the United States of America

TABLE OF CONTENTS

PUBLISHER'S NOTES i

CHAPTER 1: WHY RETIRE? 1

CHAPTER 2: HOW TO CHOOSE YOUR PLACE OF RETIREMENT? 12

CHAPTER 3: WHEN DO YOU PLAN TO RETIRE? 17

CHAPTER 4: RETIRE WITH LITTLE INCOME 22

CHAPTER 5: AMERICA'S IDEAL RETIREMENT HAVENS 29

CHAPTER 6: AMERICA'S ART COLONIES TO CONSIDER 33

CHAPTER 7: RETIRE WHERE YOUR HEART IS: HOME 39

CHAPTER 8: MEXICO, THE LAND OF ENCHANTMENT 42

CHAPTER 9: THE KINGDOM OF SPAIN 51

CHAPTER 10: THE ROMANCE OF FRANCE 56

CHAPTER 11: ITALY THE ETERNAL CITY 62

CHAPTER 12: THE CHARM OF AUSTRIA 68

CHAPTER 13: HISTORIC GREAT BRITAIN 73

CHAPTER 14: THE ISLANDS OF GREECE 79

CHAPTER 15: THE KINGDOM OF MOROCCO 86

CHAPTER 16: JAPAN, THE LAND OF THE RISING SUN 92

CHAPTER 17: HOW TO BEGIN THE JOURNEY 98

CHAPTER 18: STRATEGIES TO BE WEALTHY 106

CHAPTER 19: KEY THINGS TO REMEMBER 114

MEET THE AUTHOR 120

Publisher's Notes

Disclaimer

This publication is intended to provide helpful and informative material. It is not intended to diagnose, treat, cure, or prevent any health problem or condition, nor is intended to replace the advice of a physician. No action should be taken solely on the contents of this book. Always consult your physician or qualified health-care professional on any matters regarding your health and before adopting any suggestions in this book or drawing inferences from it.

The author and publisher specifically disclaim all responsibility for any liability, loss or risk, personal or otherwise, which is incurred as a consequence, directly or indirectly, from the use or application of any contents of this book.

Any and all product names referenced within this book are the trademarks of their respective owners. None of these owners have sponsored, authorized, endorsed, or approved this book.

Always read all information provided by the manufacturers' product labels before using their products. The author and publisher are not responsible for claims made by manufacturers.

Chapter 1: Why Retire?

This is the way the American success story is supposed to go.

A youngster gets out of school and finds himself a job in a field of work that appeals to him. He has to start pretty well at the bottom but since Samuel Lucky is a hard working, intelligent, honest lad, he slowly works his way up the ladder of success. Early in the game he finds Lois, the girl of his dreams and they marry and start up a household.

As time goes by the Luckys better their way of life. That is, at first they drove a second hand Chevrolet but after a time they graduate to a new Pontiac. Children come along and they sell their first house and buy a newer and larger one out in the suburbs in a nicer section than they could at first afford.

Most of the neighbors drive Buicks or Oldsmobile's and Mrs. Lucky complains that she isn't dressed as well as her friends and the size of their TV screen is smaller than that of the people next door. So Sam Lucky takes to bringing home work from the office in the evenings and working late into the night, and Lois gets a job as secretary in the office of the local clinic. The children are left at a nursery school part of the day.

Sam continues to bring work home and three times a week he goes to night school where he takes some pretty stiff courses to increase his worth to the firm. After awhile he gets another promotion and a raise and they can afford a new Buick, and that larger TV set, although in order to swing them Mrs. Lucky has to continue her secretarial job.

Time goes by and there are more promotions and the Luckys are able to move to a still better neighborhood, complete with Cadillac, a whole flock of super gadgets, and a maid. Lois, of course, can finally quit her job. Still later they acquire a cook and a chauffeur but in order to achieve these Mr. Lucky continues to bring home work at night. His only recreation these days is playing golf which is invariably done with company customers so that Sam can work on sales at the same time he plays. Mrs. Lucky entertains quite a bit these days—mostly the wives of executives of company customers.

By now Sam Lucky has an ulcer and Lois is going every week to her psychiatrist. The children are off in finishing and prep schools.

At the age of 65 Mr. Lucky, who is a vice president in the company now, decides to retire. They do and buy a place in Miami Beach, taking the maids, the cook and the chauffeur along with them.

Next year, at the age of 66, Sam drops dead of heart failure. He hadn't been having a very good time anyway. After forty-five years of continual work he'd forgotten how to have a good time.

That's the way the American success story is supposed to go.

But doesn't.

At least not for the overwhelming majority of us.

This is the way life is more apt to be.

A youngster gets out of school and starts looking for a job. Jim Average might have liked to have become a doctor or engineer but it didn't work out that way. For one thing, he people couldn't afford to finance eight years of pre-med and medical school. The first job that opens up for Jim is in a local print shop where they teach him to do job printing. The pay isn't too good but they tell him he's learning a trade.

He works in the print shop for a couple of years and the company puts in some new automatic equipment and Jim Average is let go. Not that he particularly cares. He never did like printing anyway. However, he's started going with Sally who works in a bakery so he needs to get another job as soon as possible. You can't get married on unemployment insurance.

The best job he can locate is clerk in a local super-market and he does his best to please a manager he can't get along with at all. He and Sally get married but since it's necessary for her to keep working if they're going to be able to live in a decent apartment and buy a car, they decide against having children.

Down through the years Jim has a series of jobs. Factory jobs, construction jobs, a job in a shipyard during the war, another print shop job. Once he and Sally even save enough money to open a service station but for one reason or other it doesn't go over and they lose all the money they invested. Once a depression comes along and for long months the family has no work at all. They have to move in with Sally's parents who can't really afford it.

Children come in spite of planning to the contrary and Jim and Sally sit up nights trying to figure out how to make ends meet. Except for when she's carrying a baby, Sally works at full time jobs. It's the only way they can keep going at all.

Some years aren't too bad. During the war and the boom that follows, Jim does pretty well. They even make a deposit on a house and buy a bigger, flashier car. They also go into the hole for a TV set, a new refrigerator, and an electric stove. After which they sit around nights some more, worrying about what's going to happen if either of them lose their jobs.

At the age of 55 Jim stops being able to find work except such positions as night watchman or elevator operator in one of the rundown buildings in the industrial part of town. And Sally can only occasionally find employment when her health is up to it, doing housework.

At 65 Jim Average gets his Social Security money and they sell their house and move down to Southern California to retire. However, the amount of Social Security money coming in hardly pays for living on the simplest standard. They get by only because one of the children is able to send them a few dollars each month.

These may sound bitter, the above accounts, but they aren't far off the beam. In one case you have a success and in the other you have an average life.

For my money, neither of them is worth the living. If I had to make a choice I'd probably choose to be Sam Lucky rather than Jim Average, but neither of them has lived a full life. And as far as retirement is concerned, both of them wound up retired at the age of sixty-five in circumstances which neither can enjoy.

Actually, it can be a great deal tougher than even the life of Jim Average which we've painted above. At least he reached the age of sixty-five, which a good many people never do, the pace of modern life being what it is. And at least Jim was able to get jobs until he was 55, a good many find themselves on the scrap heap long before this.

And I didn't even deal with the fact that while both Jim and Sally were working, trying to make ends meet, their kids were out on the streets probably taking their master's degree in juvenile delinquency. Nor did we mention that in the life of Sam Lucky he had a fine chance of becoming an alcoholic along the way in view of the pressures upon him. Or that Mrs. Lucky, in spite of her psychiatric visits, had a strong chance of winding up in a mental institute under the tensions of her frustrated life.

We haven't dealt, either, with the probability that after the age of thirty or so there was no longer any real love between Sam and Lois nor Jim and Sally. You don't lead the kind of existence they did and still retain the affection with which you started marriage.

Never in the history of any nation have there been such a large percentage of a people in mental institutions. Never has there been such a degree of juvenile delinquency. Never have there been so many divorces. Never has there been such insecurity in the hearts of a people, and our suicide rate is second highest in the world.

We Americans, as people, by no means "have it made."

This book is devoted to those who rebel against being a Sam or Lois Lucky or a Jim or Sally Average.

It's devoted to the man or woman of whatever age, from 21 and up, who has no money but does have a burning desire to get off the modern treadmill.

Or it's devoted to the man, woman, or family having a small income and a desire to retire but a feeling they have insufficient funds with which to do it.

It's devoted to the person who wishes to see life. Who wants to travel. Who wants the stimulating experiences to be found in a free way of existence.

It's devoted to he who would relax, go fishing, go hunting, go hiking, swimming, sailing, mountain climbing. Who would enjoy life's pleasures while still young enough to enjoy them in full.

Above all it's devoted to that person, man or woman, aged 21 or aged 71 who wish to spend the balance of his life profitably. And when I say profitably I mean by following a heartfelt desire to practice an art, or to pursue a study, or to ride a hobby.

It is not devoted to that person who wakes up in the morning and goes down to a hurried breakfast and then to work. At work he spends eight hours or so, with a short lunch period during which he again bolts his food so as to get back to the job again on time. In the evening he comes home to a dinner, hurriedly prepared by a wife who either works or whose time is so taken up with the children and household duties that she too is exhausted at day's end. After dinner he sits for an hour or two watching television or perhaps going to the local bar or movie. In the morning, the same routine again. By week's end there is a day and a half or two days for relaxation, so that work can be resumed at top efficiency on Monday. For two or three weeks each year the family can pile into the car and dash off on a hurried tour of some national park, or an attempt at rest in some mountain or beach resort. Then back to the grind again. Year in, year out, and the best that can be hoped for is occasional raises in pay—and that a recession or lay off will not come to steal one's livelihood.

I repeat, this book is not for the person who will exist in such a way of life. If any reader has got this far and still subscribes to such an existence, I say right now that he might as well read no further. He will never see eye to eye with me and is wasting his time. If this sort of existence is supposed to be the American Dream, I say it is not a dream but a nightmare.

And to him who complains that what I say is against the American way of life, that our people must live in this manner and that it is the best way of life. That we owe a duty to our fellow man, or our country, or the world in which we live to live such an existence. To him I pound on the table top and shout that it is not so.

The greatest men that the world has ever produced did not, could not, live such a life. No great scientific discovery, no great work of art, no great book, ever came from a man or woman who remained in such a rut.

Man makes his great discoveries; he leads a good and full life; he enjoys and gives enjoyment; only when he has leisure and the opportunity to develop himself.

Lord Byron, Shelley and Keats were great poets. But they never would have written verse had they spent their lives in the textile mills of Manchester.

From Phidias to Picasso there has never been a great artist except those who had freedom to pursue their art, who had the ability to escape, by whatever means, from the drudgery of life which besets ninety-nine out of a hundred of us.

The great inventions, the great scientific discoveries of our world have been made by men who were able to pursue their driving interests in freedom from an eight hour day or more devoted to drudgery.

What musical composer could have worked in his off hours, after a grueling day on a meaningless treadmill? What philosopher could have spun his theories after sitting at a desk working in an advertising agency trying to make people buy things they didn't really want with money they didn't really have?

But we need not be poets, writers, painters, scientists or philosophers to want and need a life free of drudgery and worry. No man can enjoy the potentials nature has awarded him without freedom from the pressure of modern existence. He must escape, he must free himself from the rut in which most are sunk, and he must get off the treadmill.

The best manner in which a man or woman can serve the society to which they belong is to be happy and at peace with themselves. You cannot make others happy unless you yourself have achieved happiness. The persons who are best suited to making this a better world are those who have achieved serenity and peace of mind.

CASE HISTORY No. 1. Perhaps the happiest person this writer has ever met was Harvey White who died a few years ago in Woodstock, New York. There must have been literally hundreds of artists, writers, composers, musicians, actors and other artists who mourned his going, not to speak of hundreds of the less talented whose lives he had affected. Harvey never had a great deal of money but he had achieved a way of life that contented him and he managed to spread his good will to almost everyone with whom he came in contact.

While still a young man he bought up a tract of several hundred acres of cheap land in the Maverick section of what was later to become the artist colony of Woodstock in the Catskill Mountains.

Friends bought other sections and practicing artists and students were invited to enjoy the advantages of this bargain paradise. And at that time, bargain paradise Woodstock was although located only a hundred miles north of New York City.

As time went by, Harvey White added small cabins to his property, usually building them himself or with the aid of local friends. He built a simple summer theatre too, and a concert theatre. Remember, he had little money but lots of friends. And what money his various projects did bring in, went to increase the size of his little colony, not into some of the necessities of life. Harvey never bothered, for instance, even to bring plumbing into his own cottage.

When I met him, I was a boy in my late teens. He taught me to print on the little press he used to put out a literary weekly and to do up programs for his concert theatre and little play house. He also taught me the value of serenity and that the most important thing in life was to enjoy it to the utmost and to try and bring enjoyment to those about us.

Harvey was interested in people who were interested in things. He didn't care what it was, but if you burned with interest in one of the arts, or politics (any shade would do, although Harvey wasn't particularly interested himself), or science, or whatever, Harvey respected you. If an artist was broke, but really working at his art, Harvey would "rent" him a cabin. Rents were ridiculously low, but somehow Harvey never got around to collecting it unless you had just sold a painting or something. Often, indeed, when he knew one of his tenants was up against it he'd drop around causally with a basket of groceries, or perhaps a cash loan.

But the thing that will stick in my mind forever was one time when I went over to his place, my mind beset by my teenage troubles, and, of course, troubles at that age are just as real as those later in life. Harvey, who looked something like Walt Whitman, was stretched out on the ground in his front yard, his head propped against a fallen log. It was a beautiful mid-summer day and he was enjoying the sun. A chipmunk played about him. He said easily, "Hi, Bob. Stretch out."

So I stretched out, immediately relaxing in his relaxing presence. Without a word being spoken, already my troubles were the less. Finally he said, "How are things going?" And I thought about that for awhile and finally I said, "All right, I guess." So we went back to silence and contemplation of a beautiful sunny day.

Just then a flashy car approached and stopped in front of the house. It was a monstrously big thing. Out of it stepped a young man dressed in the latest and the loudest of Hollywood type apparel. From Harris Tweed sport jacket to custom made suede shoes, he was the most. Harvey looked up and said interestedly, "Hi, Jimmy. Haven't seen you for a long time. Stretch out."

Jimmy looked at the ground worriedly, then took out a hanky and dusted off the tree stump before sitting on it. Harvey said, "It's good to see you again, Jimmy. Where've you been?"

Jimmy said hesitantly, "Well, I've been out on the West Coast."

"Oh? Getting any composing done? How's that opera of yours going?"

Jimmy said, "Well, no. I have a job with Paramount, Harvey. Doing arrangements for musical comedies, that sort of thing."

With real distress in his voice now, Harvey came to one elbow and said, "Golly, Jimmy, you don't have to do that. You can always come back here. I can always find one of my cabins for you!"

This is typical of Harvey White. He just couldn't imagine anybody wanting to get into the Hollywood rat-race.

I would estimate that hundreds of the American painters, writers and other artists who have achieved success in the United States today have been influenced to a greater or lesser extent by this man. He himself had achieved peace of mind, serenity and happiness in his own way, and in achieving it for himself couldn't help but spread it to others. Not only was Harvey White the happiest man I've ever met but probably the one with the most goodness in his heart.

I don't contend that everyone could, or even should, try to live life the way Harvey White did. Each must work out his own way of life. But Harvey is certain proof to me that the good life can be led without being part and parcel of today's rat-race.

Chapter 2: How to Choose Your Place of Retirement?

This book is going to show you how you can attain the good life. It's going to give scores of examples of others, including this writer, who have done it. I don't care what your educational background is or how much money you have in the bank, or if you have any at all. I don't care how old you are, or whether or not you have any skills. This thing can be done. You can retire from the rat-race, and I'm going to prove it.

If you have some savings to help out, fine. If you have a pension, no matter how small, wonderful. If you have a skill, swell. If you're a teacher, very well indeed; if you're an artist, or would like to be, or a writer, or would like to be, excellent. If you have any kind of industrial know-how, or construction skill, or if you're handy with tools, great.

Any of these things will help—but none of them are necessary. And all of this I'm going to prove. I'm going to take you by hand, and step by step, show you how to do it.

Meanwhile, however, I want to set some background. Otherwise much of what I've already said in the last chapter and much of what I will say after this one, will seem nonsense. So bear with me while I cover this subject of WHERE.

Let's face it. More than four out of every five people living in our country live in unfortunately grim surroundings.

The world is literally full of wonderful, desirable places high which to reside. But rather than seek them out the overwhelming majority of us live in such traps of humanity as New York City, Chicago, Philadelphia, Detroit, Baltimore, Cleveland, St. Louis, Washington, Boston, Pittsburgh, Milwaukee or Houston. And I've not even mentioned such real holes as Gary, East St. Louis, the coal towns of West Virginia, the textile towns of New England.

And even in our more attractive cities such as Los Angeles, San Francisco, New Orleans and Miami, the majority of the citizenry live in such poor neighborhoods, in such comparative squalor, that the basic attractiveness of the town is lost to them.

It is true enough that even New York or Chicago can be attractive and have their desirable attributes if you have the income of a millionaire but for the average reader of this book such cities mean drab living, too much heat in the summer, too much cold in the winter and sickening carbon monoxide fumes all year round. They also mean high cost of living, even though the living is poor indeed.

Is it hard for you to believe that there are places in the world, even within the boundaries of our own country, where it is possible to live quite well on what rent alone would come to in New York City? We'll come to this and prove it in following pages. Can you conceive of living in a villa on the sea with a full time servant, or possibly even two, all your meals and entertainment paid for, on what it costs to maintain an automobile in Los Angeles? This too we'll prove.

One of the great advantages of being very wealthy is the mobility that becomes yours. Where the average American spends his life in one city, and probably even in one neighborhood, only getting away for quick vacations or occasional business trips of one sort or another, the wealthy are continually on the move. They have both the money and the leisure time to indulge themselves in travel.

Thus a wealthy family can spend their winters in Miami or Palm Beach. But when the Floridian summer is upon them and the heat becomes oppressive, they leave the South and take off for the beauties of New England in the spring. If Old Sol burns too hot, this year, then it's off to Canada on a fishing trip, or up into the mountains for the cooler resorts. If this routine begins to pall, there is always the Caribbean in the winter months, a cruise to Haiti or Trinidad. Or there is Europe with all its resorts, both winter and summer.

It leads to a fuller life, a more complete life, a more educational one or, if your family of wealth doesn't particularly like travel but rather wishes to settle down, it can choose the beauty spots of the world, California, Florida, the Southwest, including Arizona, New Mexico and parts of Texas. Often they leave the States completely and establish homes on the French Riviera, the Spanish Costa del Sol, or in Paris, Rome or London if cultural pursuits are of interest.

The point we're leading up to is this. It isn't necessary to be rich to enjoy these things.

Wealth is not needed to travel and certainly not needed to live abroad, or in the most desirable parts of our own country.

It is being done by hundreds of thousands of Americans who have had the determination to get off the treadmill and to lead a full life in retirement from the rat-race. For the amount of money that it costs to buy a new automobile today you could live two or three years in comfort in some of the most beautiful places in the world.

In the body of this book I am going to list a good many of these spots and give detailed information about them. However, for right now let me throw a few quick facts at you that might set you back on your heels. That's what we need, so many of us, to be set back on our heels with facts. We need it so that we can be shocked to the point of at last standing up on our feet, showing determination and making a better life for ourselves.

We've all heard of "bargain paradises" where a couple can live for on next to nothing in adequate comfort and even a certain luxury.

They exist! Don't think they don't.

And don't think that what I say is something that applied five years or ten years ago but that in these days of inflation it is no longer so. It is so, now, today!

There are towns, cities, villages and resorts in Mexico, Spain, Austria, Greece, North Africa, Latin America, Portugal and even such exotic places as Turkey, Iraq and the South Sea Islands where living in comfort and even luxury is possible for a pittance.

That you can buy a brand new car in several different European countries for less than five thousand dollars? That in tax free Rhodes, one of the most beautiful of the Greek islands, you can buy a German camera cheaper than in Germany, Swiss watches cheaper than in Switzerland, French luxury perfumes cheaper than in France?

Of course, living abroad isn't always suitable, even for we who have decided to make the break and retire from the way of life of the majority to seek happiness, peace and serenity, rather than the carrot on the end of a stick which so many are chasing. If one has children, there is school to be considered. Or there are sometimes other motivations. However, one doesn't have to go abroad to find bargain paradises. Given a correct frame of mind, and a concentration upon the real values you can find them without the bounds of our own land.

I don't suggest that there is anywhere in the United States where you can live on a keeping up-with-the-Joneses basis for a hundred dollars a month. I don't know of any. I do know of many scenically beautiful, climatically wonderful places where life is easy, clothing informal, housing comfortable rather than luxurious and people judged by their real worth rather than the size of their bankroll or car. In such places either on a pension, or at a job or business which doesn't interfere with the good life, you can retire and live at your ease, pursuing whatever it is that really counts in your life, be it hobby, study, art, or just plain fun.

Nor is it necessary to select one spot and take roots there. Remember what I've said about the advantage of the wealthy in having mobility. This might apply to many of our readers, as it once did to me. I spent several years looking over this old world of ours. When I found a delightful spot, I'd settle for a time. It might be in the mountains here, or a river there, on the beach, or in a large cultural center such as Paris. Always I sought the beauty spots, the economical places—and always I found it simple to maintain myself. But this we will get into in succeeding chapters.

Chapter 3: When Do You Plan to Retire?

Do you know what the word vicarious means? My dictionary puts it this way:

Vicarious, adjective. 1. Performed, exercised, received or suffered in place of another. 2. Taking the place of another person or thing; acting or serving as a substitute. 3. Pertaining to or involving the substitution of one for another.

For instance, if you go to a movie and watch two or three cowboys kill a hundred or so Indians, you are having a vicarious adventure. You aren't doing it yourself, but you are thrilled, excited, titillated by seeing someone else does it. When you read a love story you have a vicarious romance. You yourself aren't kissing or being kissed, but vicariously you enjoy the thrills of love.

For many years publishers specializing in travel guides have realized that the greater numbers of persons who buy their travel books are not going to actually do any traveling. They are what are known in the trade as armchair travelers. In short they are vicarious travelers. They love the thought of traveling to farm lands, the meeting of strange peoples, the seeing of the great sights of the world— but they never get around to doing it.

Personally, I have met many of these people. They will sigh in admiration at the many countries I have seen and invariably will say, "All my life I've wanted to travel but I've never been able to afford it. I don't see how you do it." Out in front of their house will often be parked a current model of one of Detroit's biggest monstrosities. With half that amount they could have taken a leisurely trip around the world. That would still leave them enough to buy a smaller car, or a used one.

They are vicarious travelers, not real ones. They don't really want to travel but just think about it, and read about it, and talk about it.

Or we might mention two friends who publish a small magazine in Florida called the Florida Opportunity Bulletin. It is full of information about retiring to Florida, or setting up a small business in Florida, or finding employment in Florida. They distribute by advertising in national publications and in newspapers in the northern cities. They have literally tens of thousands of subscribers. Most of these subscribers they find are vicarious dreamers who will never take the step. They would love to leave the coldness and drabness of their northern homes but for whatever reason doesn't. Each month they get their copy of the Bulletin and moon over it, and discuss the various Floridian cities and towns, discuss the various jobs, the business opportunities—but they never actually pull up roots and go.

All of which is a rather lengthy build-up to what I'm driving at.

This book is not meant for the vicariously inclined. There is no way that I can prevent a reader from planking down his money, taking this volume back to the safety of his room and dreaming about getting out of the rat-race and living a real life, but never getting around to doing it. We can't prevent this but we can insist that this book is not meant for such readers.

It is meant for people who truly want to get off the treadmill and retire in comfort and to enjoy a better way of life than is lived by the overwhelming majority of Americans today. We are determined to do it, if at all possible, and it is possible and this book will prove it.

The question becomes WHEN?

And the answer is NOW!

It is either now or never. If you put it off today, you will find even more reason to put it off tomorrow and a double amount of reason to put it off next month. Until finally you will find it is next year, and five years and ten and you'll look up someday and find that life has passed you by. That you've spent it dreaming about a better way of life but never quite had the courage to reach out and take it, although it was always there to take. You'll find youth gone, and many of the best things in life never realized. You will have lived and died just one sadder drop of water in an unhappy ocean.

I don't mean to suggest here that you drop this book right this minute, put your hat on your head, go down and tell the boss what he can do with his job, draw your money out of the bank, and go to the local tourist agency and buy a ticket for Italy (although, frankly, I have known people who did just that and never regretted it).

I do suggest that right this moment you decide in your own mind, and decisively, that you are going to do this thing. That you are going to get off the treadmill and start living. Decide it with determination. Burn it into your brain so definitely that it will remain there until you have accomplished it.

Then read this book right on through with extreme care. Mark every passage that applies to you so that when you are finished you can go back and restudy them. All passages of course, don't and can't apply to you. If I give an example of opportunities for female teachers in Rome working part time at enjoyable employment for high pay, it obviously doesn't apply to a male, aged 25, who has no teaching experience but is a good driver.

If I tell of a business opportunity in Southern Spain for anyone with two thousand dollars of capital, it obviously doesn't apply to someone who starts off with no capital at all. Or if I describe a beautiful spot in Greece where a couple with a pension can live in luxury for five hundred dollars a month, it obviously is of no interest to some young man or woman who wants to travel, rather than to settle down.

But mark the sections that apply to you. Perhaps there are only two or three that fit all of your requirements but, if so, there will be many others that will give you ideas which you can possibly develop.

Each reader of this book is an individual, and each has his own particular problems, so obviously there is no set blueprint for all. Each must adapt what I have to say to his own circumstances.

Read this book through thoroughly, then go over and over those case histories that apply to your age group, your sex, your marital status, your desire or lack of desire to travel, your climatic or scenic wants. Start to work thinking about them.

In the concluding chapter of the book you'll find various government publications, and other reading material recommended. By all means send for those that apply to you. Above all, we do not recommend that you go off half-cocked. Start with a cold determination that you are going to do it and then plan it well.

Nothing in this book is of more importance than that which I have just said in the past few pages. Right now, I suggest that you start back again at the beginning of this chapter and reread it. If this determination that we recommend doesn't seize you, then you may never retire in the manner that is possible.

Chapter 4: Retire With Little Income

This book is not devoted solely to persons who have established incomes, either pensions or investments. I plan to reveal how any adult American, with or without income, with or without savings, can retire and lead a more full life. However, before dealing with general details on how to accomplish this I should like to devote a short chapter to those persons who do have a small income already on hand.

I say a small income, because it is obvious that if you have a large one you have no need of my advice on how to retire, no matter what age you may be. Given sufficient money, nobody need have any difficulty retiring.

The very purpose of this book is to tell those persons who do not have sufficient money—or at least think they haven't—how they can accomplish this desirable goal.

Give a European a small income, you can almost say no matter how small, and he'll retire, no matter what his age. The average European feels that the most important thing in life is freedom to dispense his time in the way he wishes. He figures that as long as you are at the mercy of a business, even your own, or of an employer, you are not truly free. Others dictate how your time shall be spent.

So you will find throughout Europe and especially in the very economical countries such as Spain, Austria and Greece hundreds of thousands of Europeans, both single persons and families, who have retired at any age from 18 to 80. They simply cannot understand why anyone should continue working after already reaching the point where he, or she, has sufficient funds with which to lead a full life.

I know I am going to run into disbelief here, but I personally have met, in various places throughout the world, single persons, couples and even families who have retired on little income.

And when I mention families retiring on small amounts, I don't mean per person, I mean the whole family.

Of course, there are a good many more who have retired on larger sums, and any addition at all to this minimum makes considerable difference in living standards, but nevertheless, there are some who stretch out one hundred dollars a month to the point where they can retire on it.

There are hundreds of thousands of Europeans who have retired on one measly incomes. In fact, there are few, if any, European nations where the average workingman can look forward to a pension that large upon his retirement at 60 or 65 years of age.

However, it would occur to comparatively few American couples who had a guaranteed income to retire. Why should this be?

Largely because we Americans have established a set of standards which makes retirement a faraway dream. There are some who say that this set of standards is a ridiculous one, but ridiculous or not it is there.

If you feel you absolutely must have a new automobile every year or two, then obviously you are not going to be able to retire anytime soon.

If prime quality steak and fancy restaurants are a must, and a trendy wardrobe is important to you you're sunk and will probably have to keep on that treadmill for a good many more years.

It's a matter of sitting down and thinking it out. What is it that you really want in life? What is really important to you?

If you must have the ultra-ultra gadgets that our civilization has dreamed up, and then you will need a considerable income before you can retire, free of any work, because they are very expensive. In later chapters of this book I am going to illustrate ways in which you can make good money with a minimum of effort, but if you wish to retire completely free of any effort at all and still demand a king-size house, a new car, the most expensive of frozen and canned foods as well as the latest styles in clothing, you're going to have to have a whopper of an income.

However, I repeat, what is really important to you?

There is no doubt whatsoever that if you have a sufficient initial amount of money to buy a car and a trailer (it need not be new) or a motor home (it need be neither new nor large) and a modest income, you can retire and see America, Canada and Mexico.

Leisurely, thoroughly, happily. There is just no doubt at all. Tens of thousands of other Americans are doing it. You can do it too.

In Miami, to choose only one example among many, there are, thousands of persons who have chosen boats on which to retire, rather than motor homes. Hundreds of these boats are docked along the Miami River and in bays and inlets in the vicinity. They range in size from thirty-five feet upward and every type of small craft ever heard of is represented. There are sailboats and motor cruisers, houseboats and yachts.

The reason that there are so many craft in the Miami area, so low priced, is due to the nature of our so-called upper class Americans. The usual person, who can afford to buy a boat and operate it as a hobby, wouldn't be seen dead in a model that was several years old. Like their automobiles, they must show themselves off in the very latest. In short, depreciation is very rapid.

A person, couple, or small family, then, can buy these used boats at a comparative pittance. By living upon it full time, rent is saved and many of the playboy-type costs of boating are eliminated. You must pay dockage fees which will run you a monthly fee, and if you are on a budget, can't take your craft out on fishing trips or cruises as often as you might like. But even on a tight budget, life on a boat can be pleasant indeed.

Fish becomes a major item in your diet, and, particularly in Southern waters such as Miami, you will find fruits and vegetables in remarkable abundance at low price. If you have never been aboard the type craft of which I speak, I can only tell you that quarters are surprisingly ample, less constricted than a trailer, and the appointments and conveniences of the very best. Only remember that this boat which you have purchased at such a small amount was once a wealthy man's plaything.

But if neither motor home life nor life on the water appeals to you, you might consider one of the cheaper areas of our country in which to retire in a house. It is almost unbelievable, once again, the prices at which you can purchase a small house, or a small farm, here in America.

You see, seventy years ago it was still practical in our country for a family to live on forty acres of land or less and make an adequate living. Every state in the Union had tens of thousands of such small farms. However, as the agricultural revolution developed it became increasingly difficult for the small farmer, with his horse or two, his few cattle, his often-rocky fields, to make a go of it. Every year thousands of farms were given up and their occupants went off to acquire jobs in the city.

In many, many of the beauty spots of America, and I name only New England and the Ozarks of Arkansas, as two examples among the many, these farms remain—for sale at a pittance.

And not only is the initial investment on these so small, but you'll find that costs of living in general in such areas are far below those to which we are accustomed in the cities. Meats, vegetables, fruits are to be purchased from the neighbors. Chickens and perhaps a pig or two are practical to have in your own backyard. Indeed if amateur farming is of interest to you, such a hobby can pay off nicely.

I am not suggesting if you are city-bred, that you can go out and buy one of these former farms and make a full living upon it by working on a part time basis. It's been done, of course, but on an average you will find that if a farmer, born and raised on a farm, was not able to make a living on this place, neither will you be able to. But you don't have to.

Thus far, I have dealt with retiring in the United States on a minimum amount. And there will be many who have no desire to spend their lives outside the boundaries of our own country.

However, it is my own opinion that a person, or couple, that has a small income, whether it is a pension, or dividends from some investment, can stretch the amount much further by living abroad. As I have already pointed out, a dollar goes much further in such countries as Mexico, Spain, Austria and Greece, among others, than it does in the United States. In fact, the United States is one of the most expensive countries on earth, and many will tell you that it is the most expensive of all.

If you steer clear of the tourist centers, it is possible to live on a very high standard in these countries. Don't forget what I have said above in regard to the Europeans.

It becomes obvious, then, that it is possible to live on this amount. In fact, a bit of consideration shows that since the European is working to acquire his wages, and you are retired, you will have various advantages over him. He must dress for his job; he must utilize the public transportation every day going to and from work. He has expenses you won't have, including taxes, since, as you possibly know, if you live abroad for over 18 months you need not pay American income taxes.

In following chapters we will go into detail on the cheaper countries and the desirable ones in which to retire. It would be duplication to give details here.

Nor will it be necessary to give case histories of Americans who have bought motor homes or boats in which to retire. The examples are so many that we all know of them. If not, a short trip to the nearest trailer camp and a bit of conversation, will give you more basic information on the subject than I could list here on many a page.

The important thing, they must thing to remember is that the majority of us have false standards. We have been told by the greatest advertising industry the world has ever seen that we have to have this luxury, that we must have that one, that we must spend, spend, SPEND, if we wish to achieve the good life.

Nonsense! The good life is to be achieved by freeing ourselves of this very rat-race which they sponsor. And this can be done on a very small amount, if such an amount is steady and dependable.

Chapter 5: America's Ideal Retirement Havens

As we've already said, the United States is the most expensive country in the world.

However, there is a big IF to this.

Because in many respects it is the cheapest country in the world.

It is the most expensive country if you attempt to keep up with the Joneses, if you insist on big houses in expensive areas, new cars and a yearly rash of new TV sets, remodeling, technology, gadgets and what not.

However, I know of no other place in the world where you can buy a good reliable used car reasonably. And you can in America. You can get an excellent used car in our country and particularly in times of economic recession.

There is no country on earth that produces so cheaply good sturdy ready-to-wear clothing. A pair of American denims will outwear anything selling abroad for a comparable price, two or three times over.

Even food. True enough if you go into the super-market and buy filet mignon, you'll pay plenty. But if you have made a study of living economically and have learned to cook delicious dishes from the cheaper cuts of meat, you have it made in the United States like nowhere else. There is no place of which I know where chicken is cheaper and better than in America. It's a premium priced meat all over Europe. And did you know that in Europe tongue, heart, liver, brains, tripe, sweetbreads and particularly kidneys are premium priced? In many parts of our country these are used for dog and cat food, or even thrown away.

No, you can live cheaply and well in the United States if you make a hobby of it. If you seek out the cheaper sections of the nation and then pull every economy trick in the game.

The term bargain paradise is becoming increasingly popular these days as more and more people, in despair at our national way of life, search desperately for an alternative. Usually when we say bargain paradise our thoughts fly to countries beyond the horizon such as Tahiti, to Spain, to the Canary Islands, Peru, or Austria.

In fact, it may come as a surprise to some that we have many a bargain paradise right here in our own land.

The term explains itself, whether in the United States or abroad, a bargain paradise is an area where prices are low and scenery and climate are superlative. It's as simple as that.

And where are there such places in the United States?

All over.

New England, back away from the cities. For those, in particular, who demand the changes in season New England (and up-state New York) is one of the most beautiful sections of our country.

The coastal areas between Maryland and Florida offer hundreds of miles of picturesque beaches. These areas can provide loads of fishing, swimming, and boating. The further south you go, of course, the warmer the climate.

Florida, ruling out only the larger cities and the swank tourist resorts, is one big bargain paradise. It's cheap, it's beautiful. Its offerings are boundless to the retired sportsman or sportswoman.

The Gulf Coast between Florida and New Orleans is cheap, warm, and wonderful.

The Rio Grande Valley, and in particular the lower stretch in the vicinity of McAllen where the climate is superior even to that of Florida.

New Mexico, Arizona, Southern Colorado are for those who love mountains, desert and wasteland. These states offer the glories of the West—and are bargain priced if you stay away from the population and tourist centers.

California, Oregon, Washington but always avoid the big cities and resorts, of course. Los Angeles and San Francisco can be as expensive as any city in the country, but little Northern cities, tucked up in the High Sierras, is a bargain paradise indeed.

The Ozarks of Arkansas and Missouri are rapidly becoming one of the more popular bargain paradises, especially for those who wish a small farm on which to retire.

Research is a key stroke away and has never been easier. Do your homework and make a plan.

Chapter 6: America's Art Colonies to Consider

The art colony is an interesting institution peculiar not only to the United States. In fact, you find them even more often in Mexico and Europe, and for all I know all over the world where there are artists. Since retiring from the grind, I have personally lived in such art colonies in America, Mexico, Spain, Italy and Morocco. And always I've found stimulating qualities in both the towns and their populations.

When I say artist, I don't, of course, mean just painters. Your art colonies will attract the practitioners of every art in the book— and some not in the book. There will be painters, sculptors, writers, composers, actors, photographers, musicians, handicraft practitioners and what not. Above all there will be large numbers of pseudo-artists who do a great deal of talking, cocktail in hand, about painting or writing, or whatever, but very little real work. And then there will be even larger numbers of folk who like to hang around artists and consider themselves intellectuals, whatever that means.

But in spite of the large number of phonies to be found in the average art colony they still have their fascination. Usually there is an art school or two, in case you are interested yourself seriously or just as a hobby, and always there are the stimulating conversations, the strange new ideas, the heated arguments, the striving for expression.

Why and what is an art colony? Well, it usually goes something like this. An artist, or group of artists, finds some cheap place in which to live, trying to locate it in a spot of scenic beauty and preferably where the weather is good. The economical part of it is a prime necessity since artists seem almost always to be short of money. Having located such a place, they write their friends and in one way and another word gets around. Here is a beauty spot, here are other artists with whom to associate, here one can get a little cabin and work at one's art very well indeed on very little money.

More artists move in, and sooner or later one of the travel magazines or art publications writes the town up, naming it an art colony. So still more people hear about the place, including the above mentioned pseudo-artists and the hangers-on. And the town begins to fill. Where formerly you could easily rent a little cabin, there is a housing shortage and rents double. Where formerly you could buy a jug of red wine (in the west) or applejack (in the east) from one of the local citizens, now a liquor store goes up. Where formerly there was a little local tavern where you sat around in the evenings having a beer or two, a flashy nightclub and two or three neon-lit bars complete with juke-boxes, take over. Where formerly you got your milk and butter, a bushel of potatoes and an occasional chicken, from one of the local farmers, now somebody opens a supermarket and it becomes the only place you can buy food.

Before you know it, the town is booming. Souvenir shops arise, swank hotels go up, and the local beanery is expanded into a garish restaurant with high prices and a French chef.

I've seen this happen more than once. Greenwich Village, in New York City, is far from cheap anymore and you have to really dig around to find a real artist there. Woodstock, up in the Cats-kills, is another example—a far cry from the days when Harvey White and his friends first started it. Taos, New Mexico, once the bargain paradise so loved by D. H. Lawrence, is now in the way of becoming a tourist trap, although it's still not too bad if you get out of town a ways. There are many other examples of art colonies that have gone to seed. The Vieux Carre in New Orleans, the beloved French Quarter, once the cheapest part of town and by far the most picturesque, is now a combination of honky tonks, tourist traps, and souvenir stores. And, above all, it's become so expensive that few artists can afford to live there.

Laguna Beach and Carmel, in California; Provincetown on Cape Cod in Massachusetts; Boothbay Harbor, Maine; all in their time were ultra-economical beauty spots that attracted the artists by droves. And now they're prohibitively expensive tourist centers, the streets full of gawking visitors hoping to catch sight of a "real Bohemian," whatever that is.

But the artist has a defense against all this. He can always move on to another place, form a new colony. And that's what usually happens. Few art colonies last more than ten or twenty years from the time they are first founded.

Today a great many of our painters, writers and the others are streaming abroad to such art colonies as San Miguel Allende and Ajijic, in Mexico, Torremolinos in Spain, and Positano in Italy, although Italy is by no means inexpensive these days.

But in spite of this trend to move abroad, there are still a good many art colonies in the United States and in every section of the country from Cape Cod in New England to Sarasota in Florida and from Colorado Springs and Taos in the Rockies to Laguna Beach and Carmel on the Pacific. If not every State then certainly every section of the country has its art colony. Some of them will support literally hundreds of artists, genuine as well as the psuedo variety; some will have no more than a dozen or so.

What is the advantage in living in an art colony? Of retiring in such a place?

There are various advantages for some types of people.

If you are interested in the arts yourself and particularly if you have ambitions along this line, the advantages are obvious. You will find others to help you, give you pointers, instruct you. But even though you have no desire to practice any of the arts yourself, you might still find enjoyment in the atmosphere that prevails in an art colony.

A feature desirable to many is the complete informality. Usually, you'll find that denims are the standard dress. Clothing in general is not something you have to worry about. Your fellow man in an art colony is more interested in what you think and do than he is in how you look.

Nor are there pretentions about your house. If you have a little two or three room shack and do your own cooking on a two burner stove, and serve nothing better than dago-red in the way of refreshments to your guests, it's not going to keep even the most successful artist or writer in town from coming to your parties. The only thing that counts at a party in an art colony is the quality of the conversation because although conversation is an art rapidly disappearing in our country, it certainly is not in the art colony. Here it still reigns supreme.

The last thing in the world that people will care about is the age of your car (or whether or not you have one at all), the clothes you wear, the food you eat or the house in which you live. They are more apt to turn up their noses at you if you spend a great deal of time watching TV or lost in a computer, .rather than subjects on art, politics, and world affairs.

There is one other element in living in art colonies that perhaps has a snobbish sound to it, but is very real to many people. In your usual way of life, assuming that you are an average American with an average job and income, you are not apt to have the opportunity of meeting the celebrities of the world. Even though you may be interested in writing (or reading) it is unlikely you will ever meet Hemingway, even though he might come to the city in which you live. Even though you may be interested in art, and even paint a bit yourself, it is unlikely that you will ever meet Picasso. Even though you are interested in the theatre it is unlikely that you will meet the big name actors, or even a movie star or so. Not if you're the average American.

However, in the art colony the barriers go down.

I am not a "celebrity hunter" myself although I have found that usually those persons who become celebrities as a result of their work are of more than usual interest. However, during the length of only one summer while I was living in the art colony of Torremolinos, Spain, I met among many others MacKinley Kantor, who won the Pulitzer prize with his novel Andersonville that year; Paul Lucas, the movie star, lived next door to me; Dominguin, currently the world's top matador, came to a couple of parties I also attended; Ben Stahl, one of America's outstanding painters, became a friend of mine; Count Felix Von Luckner, the "Sea Devil" of World War One, was about town; William P. McGivern, one of the top mystery writers, and Maureen Daly, his wife, who is famous for such books as Seventeenth Summer, were also good friends.

British writer Alec Waugh was also around and Baron Wrangle, who never wears that patch he has in the Hathaway shirt ads in public. And, oh yes, one night when I was having a quiet drink in El Remo Prince Rainer and Grace Kelly came in for dinner and a mutual friend introduced us—although I haven't the vaguest idea why. I suppose he thought that everybody would like the opportunity of meeting Grace and her prince.

But that's the way it is in an art colony. Complete informality, no one better than anyone else. If a celebrity comes to town, no matter what field he might be in, you'll meet him at one of the local parties, one of the local bars, or possibly sitting around on the beach or at a sidewalk cafe. This, of course, applies to American art colonies as well as European ones.

Chapter 7: Retire Where Your Heart Is: Home

We make a big point in this book of not only the need to retire while still young enough to enjoy it, but also of seeking out the better places in the world in which to appreciate the very tops in climatic and scenic offerings. However, it is obvious that many of us are, for various reasons, in no position to leave our present homes.

For one thing, perhaps you are already living in one of the land's bargain paradises. Perhaps your home is already in Florida, Southern California, Arizona, or the Lower Rio Grande Valley. Why leave? Why not retire where you are already?

In fact, there are often advantages in simply retiring in your own home town. Possibly you have a house already paid for, and undoubtedly you have a good many connections, not to speak of friends and relatives. Very possibly your credit is good at the bank, to start a retirement project.

And, of course, there may be many reasons why you cannot just get up and go—as I did—leaving the old world behind you. Possibly you have aged parents depending upon your presence. Perhaps you have children in the local schools, and hesitate to take them from their friends and classes.

But whatever the reason, this chapter is devoted to the reader who wishes to retire but is in no position to leave the home in which he now resides.

The purpose of this book is more to get you in the frame of mind to take this retirement step. To show you examples of others who have done it successfully. To give you that little push that will result in your getting off the treadmill and making a more satisfactory way of life.

But there is one thing I'd like to stress in this matter of retiring in your own home town. If you packed your things one day, collected whatever savings you had, and took off for Sarasota, Florida; Truckee, California; or Santé Fe, New Mexico, and once there started your new way of life, there would be nobody to look you askance. It would seem completely natural to them, as would any project you might develop in order to augment your income.

Ah, but in your own home town. What would they say if you quit your job? Your job as foreman down at the pretzel bending department of the biscuit company, where your father worked before you and his father before him. Would they think you'd gone stark raving mad when you announced that although you were only

25 years of age, you had decided to retire from the rat-race? Would the minister of your church come around to discuss it with you? Would relatives ranging from your parents to second cousins attempt to argue you out of it—contending that the natural state of man is slavery in a factory or office?

In short, would you be able to stand the guff from people who probably deep within themselves would love to do just what you've decided to do, but haven't the courage. And since they haven't the courage themselves they don't want you to have it. The mob instinct seems to be to hate anybody not exactly like the members of the mob.

We Americans have long prided ourselves on being "rugged individualists." Supposedly, we are all "rugged individualists." Perhaps it's just an optical illusion that the overwhelming majority seem to be just the opposite. Far from an individualist, rugged or otherwise, the average American today does not seem capable of standing up on his hind legs and asserting himself. He is scared to death of losing his little job, and the modicum of pseudo-security it gives him. That this situation will someday end, and that soon, I believe and hope, but right now the average American is using little effort to get him off the horrible treadmill he is running upon.

So! Let them talk. Let them sneer, if sneer they will. They'd like to be doing just what you're doing—escape from the rat-race— but they haven't the guts.

Chapter 8: Mexico, the Land Of Enchantment

In a nutshell. The Federal Republic of Mexico with its area of 760,373 square miles and its population pushing the third largest nation of North America (following Canada and the United States) but the second largest in population.

Considering the fact that she is an immediate neighbor of ours, it is astonishing how many misconceptions Americans who have never been to Mexico have acquired. Perhaps this is because the least colorful, the least desirable sections of this fascinating country are right on our border and directly across from Texas, New Mexico, Arizona and California. In fact, the traveler has to proceed several hundred miles into the interior before he finds what could be called the "real Mexico."

If I had to spend the rest of my life in any one country and couldn't choose my own, I think it would be Mexico that I selected. There is certainly no other country I have seen in the world that offers so much in the way of the enjoyable things of life. She has scenic beauty to rival anything in Switzerland; her climate tops by far that of Spain, Italy and Greece; her food rivals that of any European land save France, and any Oriental country save China; her historic monuments are surpassed only by Egypt; the variety of her countryside is rivaled nowhere from the deserts of the north, to the cool plateaus of her central sections, to the jungles of Yucatan. You can ski in summer, if you wish, or swelter in winter. Or you can abide in such high altitude towns as Cuernavaca or Guanajuato, where the tropical climate is cooled by the seven thousand feet that they are above sea level. Here you will not be comfortable wearing your sport jacket in August, nor will you need more in January.

Only a few years ago Mexico was comparatively unknown to us Americans from the United States. The majority of us had a vague picture which involved Pancho Villa, played by Wallace Beery, dashing over the countryside, shooting and burning, and sneering at "the gringos." We thought of Mexico as backward, her people barefooted peons a hundred years behind the "civilized" nations of the world.

But then a change began to come over us. Our art students returning from Europe informed us that in Paris and Rome the most famous "American" artists were not from the United States, as far as opinion in Europe was concerned, but were Rivera, Orozco, Siqueiros and Tamayo, from Mexico. Occasional visitors south of the border returned with the information that Mexico City was one of the most cosmopolitan and beautiful large cities in the world.

And then, following the war, we began to hear in earnest of the cheap prices. Why, you could live in a fabulous beauty spot for less than a hundred a month!

So we began to visit this land to our south. First a trickle, then a stream of tourists, and then a fabulous rush which is still taking place. As in any land which enjoys (or suffers, according to how you look at it) a tourist boom, certain cities became centers of tourism and prices there zoomed. Such places as Acapulco, famed Pacific coast beach resort, quickly became almost as expensive as Florida or California. Cuernavaca, just south of Mexico City, became a city of retired wealthy folk, sky-high in price by Mexican standards. Mexico City itself began to feel the boom and American style apartments and houses upped in price.

But tourists have a tendency to get in a rut. Like ants, they follow blindly their leaders, speed madly along the same paths. The real Mexico, the Mexican Mexico, the beautiful Mexico, the economical Mexico, is still there—off the tourist routes. All of which we intend to prove in this chapter.

I can say without hesitation that there is no country in the world more suited for the average American to retire in than Mexico. If you have a small pension or income, you will find it as cheap as any place where you can enjoy gracious living. If you wish to take up part time work or start a little business deal of your own, here too Mexico offers as many opportunities as any. The country is booming.

There is another great advantage. Mexico is so available that you can experiment there. Whatever your present occupation, you can take off a little time, run down to Mexico and "case" the situation. Find the town you like. Find your own niche. Get your project under way—if it's a project that you have in mind.

THE MEXICANS. Just as we Americans have had a misconception of Mexico, thinking it a land of desert, rather than of fabulous beauty, so we have had a poor picture of the Mexican people. Possibly this is because the Mexicans we have come in contact with most in our own country were the poorest elements to be found among them. Each year tens of thousands of Mexicans cross the border to work in our fields. Obviously these are no more the average Mexican that our migrant farm workers are the average American.

Mexicans, like us, differ greatly. The educated Mexican of Mexico City is a cultured, progressive person and very possibly took his schooling in an American or European university, although many Mexican schools are excellent. The University of Mexico, just south of Mexico City, is the most outstanding in Latin America.

To the other extreme are the natives—you might almost say savages—who live in the jungles of the interior in Yucatan, Quintana Roo and Campeche. They exist much as did their ancestors before the coming of the Spaniards, even the bow and arrow being in daily use.

Between these two extremes is the average Mexican. Proud of his country and its revolutionary traditions, he is the most courteous person in the world. He is also generous, a great lover of his family, hard working (in spite of all of our "siesta" jokes to the contrary), loyal to his friends, and hospitable to strangers.

And above all, he is picturesque. There is nothing in Europe to equal the Mexican fiesta. The costume, the fireworks, the dancing and music in the streets. All over Mexico are dancing clubs, somewhat similar to our "square dance societies" which keep alive the dances of the Aztecs, Mayans and other pre-conquest Mexican peoples.

To think of the Mexican as an ignorant, shifty-eyed, untrustworthy "greaser" is as silly as to picture the average Russian as black bearded and with a bomb in each hand.

MONEY. One of the reasons why Mexico is so very cheap for Americans is the excellent exchange between peso and dollar. In many commodities you will find a peso will buy almost what a dollar will in our own country.

As the international finance expression goes, the peso is "pegged" to the dollar. The United States supports the peso, in other words, and on the money market in Switzerland and Tangier if the dollar goes up so does the peso and vice versa. There is no advantage then in attempting to buy pesos at cut rates on the money markets. Yet get as good an exchange in a Mexican bank as you will anywhere.

If you plan to work or open a business in Mexico, you should plan on achieving immigrate status which takes a period of five years in all, during which you have to spend at least nine months a year in Mexico. This has nothing to do with losing your American citizenship, it is just a matter of becoming a permanent resident of Mexico and achieving all rights of citizens of Mexico except the right to vote or participate in politics.

With inmigrado status you need no work permit. Without such status you can still work if you get a permit. Such permits are issued if the company that wants you can prove to the government that a Mexican can't handle the job. For instance, we had a friend in Acapulco who was an American cook. He got a wonderful job teaching the Mexican cooks in the swank Acapulo hotels and restaurants how to cook American dishes. No trouble getting a permit at all.

You can also make money in Mexico, if the money comes from without the country. That is, suppose you started a little ceramics business in the area around Lake Patzcuaro, from whence comes some of Mexico's best pottery. If all your ceramics were sent up to the United States and dollars came back, then the Mexican government certainly has no argument with you.

PARTICULARLY RECOMMENDED LOCALITIES. Mexico has so much to offer in desirable climate, scenic beauty, cities and towns, that it is largely a matter of your own taste.

If only a city can please you, then realize that Mexico City is one of the most beautiful in the world, often compared to Paris, and has a population of approximately seven million which makes it one of the largest in the Western Hemisphere. The cheapest really large city of which I know, Mexico City still has all of the advantages of the metropolis. Theatres, museums, restaurants, modern shops, night clubs, libraries, schools. Its climate is superb seeing that it is in the tropics but nestled 7,500 feet in the mountains.

Or you have the smaller towns, also in the mountains, or the wonderful fishing towns along both coasts, such as Manzanillo which has many similarities to Acapulco, further south, but is comparatively untouched by Americans or other foreigners. Prices are lower than average, fishing is wonderful, and the seafood including lobsters, crabs, and turtles is simply out of this world.

If you're artistically inclined, and particularly like to associate with your fellow Americans, the Lake Chapala area might be for you. Very cheap, very artistic, several little towns to choose from, the most popular of which is Ajijic.

If you prefer not to go too far from the States, but are still inclined to the "away from it all" dream, you might consider Alamos, a former silver center with mansions and palaces galore from the days when Mexican silver supplied the world. For a time almost a ghost city, Alamos is making a comeback through Americans who have drifted down. It's located only a couple of hundred miles or so south of Nogales, Arizona.

But my personal favorites are San Miguel de Allende, where I lived off and on for eighteen months, and Merida, Yucatan, for me one of the most charming cities in the world and one of the more remote.

San Miguel, which I've already described to some extent above, is an old Spanish Colonial town and so attractive that the Mexican government has made it a national monument. The streets are cobbled, no signs, neon or otherwise, are allowed and no changes can be made in a building without government permission. No new houses can go up until approved as not conflicting with the town architecture.

Some years ago an art school was begun in San Miguel and for a time was extremely successful. However a scandal arose and the school lapsed to be followed not long afterward by the present Instituto Allende which teaches just about every art and handicraft ever thought of and at cut rate prices. There are a good many artists of all types in San Miguel besides those at the school. In fact, it is estimated that approximately 1000 Americans either practicing the arts or interested in them are present at San Miguel at any one time.

The presence of so many Americans has led to the establishment of an English book store, the presence of American canned foods and American drugs, and to the coming of English speaking doctors and dentists. American movies can be seen at the local theatres.

Although 7,000 feet high in the mountains of Guanajuato, you have year around swimming since there is a hot springs a short ways out of town. There are two pools, one extremely hot, one pleasantly warm.

Mexico City is approximately two hundred miles to the south over good roads. In fact, some of the local bullfights fans drive down in the morning every Sunday and then, after the fight, drive back home that night.

But as pleasant as I found San Miguel de Allende and as much as I loved living there, I believe that if I were to return to Mexico I would wish to live this time in Merida, or Progresso, in Yucatan.

Although Merida, Yucatan's capital, is one of Mexico's larger cities it is practically unknown to the average Mexican—not to speak of the average tourist. This is because although Yucatan is a Mexican state, it is cut off from the balance of the country by all but impenetrable jungle. It is possible to get to Merida by land by using a combination of train and road, but it is a difficult expedition taking the better part of a week. Instead, for years the usual method of reaching Merida was by boat from Vera Cruz to Progresso and thence by road to Merida. Now, the airlines use Merida as a stopping point winging their way south, and this is the most popular tourist method of arriving in the country.

Cut off like this Merida gets few tourists and as a consequence has built up a culture of its own in many ways dissimilar to the Mexican way of life further north. Then too, the Mayan Indians are considerably different in appearance than those nearer Mexico City.

Prices are so nearly the same as elsewhere in Mexico that I shall not comment upon them, but I must point out that here fishing and hunting are supreme. The jungles are so thick that it would be impossible to hunt them out and consequently game is available at all times. Venison is on the menu every meal of the day, in every restaurant, and the Mayans have developed some venison dishes I've never seen elsewhere.

Food in general is all but free, so lavishly does the tropical climate supply it. And as generous as is the land, so is the sea. Sea food such as is to be found in the markets of Merida is unrivaled elsewhere in quantity and in quality.

For the student, the fabulous ruins left by the Mayan civilizations are everywhere and awesome in their beauty. Some architects are of the opinion that the House of the Governors, in Uxmal, is as beautiful a building as man ever erected, not excepting even the Parthenon of Athens.

I might mention that since Yucatan is so seldom visited by foreigners, Americans or otherwise, the people are even more hospitable than usual. An American in Merida, or Progresso, thinking in terms of a permanent or semi-permanent stay, and looking about for a business opportunity or an easy going job, should have few difficulties in supplying his wants. He would find fewer Americans about, with whom to associate, than he would in Ajijic or San Miguel de Allende, but, on the other hand he would find fewer competitors in his attempts to make a good living the easy way. In fact, he might very well start up one or more of the projects that are already in full swing in these more northern towns.

CHAPTER 9: THE KINGDOM OF SPAIN

IN A NUTSHELL. For some reason most of we Americans who have never visited Spain think of this country as a small one and it comes as a shock to find that of all of our States only Texas and Alaska is larger than she.

Possibly our ignorance of Spain is due to the fact that few members of this generation have visited Spain. Her civil war broke out in 1936 and didn't end until 1939. Hardly was it over but the Second World War began and for nearly seven years Europe was wrapped in conflict and tourism was a forgotten luxury. Both Spanish and American officials are trying to ignore the fact now but Spain was, and is, a fascist country and during the war she supported the Axis Powers. This undoubtedly helped, when the war was over, to keep American tourists from the country. For years Spain was virtually ignored.

Tourists were coming to Europe as never before, but the main points of interest were further north, England, France, Switzerland,

Italy. In 1947 only 3,700 of our countrymen entered Spain and the figure only slightly more than doubled in 1948.

But finances have been chaotic since the war and everywhere prices have literally zoomed. France, once a bargain paradise, became as expensive as the United States, or nearly so. And Switzerland and Italy trailed not far behind. Rumors began to drift up from the south that Spain was still operating at pre-war prices. That you could travel in Spain at a fraction the price in the more popular tourist countries, or could retire on a pittance.

And nothing spreads so fast in the traveling set, and those who live permanently, or semi-permanently abroad as such rumors. Thousands began to drift into Spain, and then tens of thousands, until at this writing at least a million Americans visit Spain each year, and thousands have become permanent residents.

Of course, just because a country is cheap is no reason to retire there. But Spain offers a good deal more than economy. Her scenery is varied, her climate probably the best in Europe, with the possible exception of the Greek islands, there is a wide Anglo-American population which guarantees companionship if you cannot find it among the Spaniards, and the luxuries as well as the necessities of life is available.

THE SPANIARDS. It is possible to type a people such as the Swiss or the Danes with a certain amount of accuracy but when you take a country as large as Spain it becomes as difficult as it would be to type the American. Obviously all Americans aren't the same—neither are all Spaniards.

In Andulusia in the south, for instance, live the gypsies and although I have no prejudices in matters of race, nationality, or color I think I can truly state that the Spanish gypsy is the dirtiest, most poverty stricken, most dishonest, most untrustworthy people

I have met in Europe, certainly they are the most lazy and shiftless. To the other extreme you have the residents of Madrid and also the Catalans of Barcelona who are modern, aggressive, hard working, honest folk who differ comparatively little from the average American.

Personally, I like the average Spaniard. I find him honest; clean, to the extent his poverty allows him to be; hospitable far beyond the extent he can afford; in love with his country, but with an amazing lack of knowledge about the rest of the world; a lover of his family, but also of good wine and good food, not to speak of good folk music. He is also, in spite of all misinformation to the contrary a hard worker (except for the gypsies).

MONEY. Spain has one of the softest currencies in Europe. Just know that the peseta fluctuates greatly.

PRICES. As we've stated above, Spain is currently the cheapest country in Europe. It is still quite possible to live comfortably on a very modest income. Adding to your income, even just a little bit sends your standard of living up very rapidly. Doubling it puts you in a living standard group probably considerably higher than the average American's what with a really large home and two or more servants. What would be considered "low-income" in America is real wealth in Spain. You could easily live like a Spanish Don and his Senorita.

PARTICULARLY RECOMMENDED LOCALITIES. Spain has a score or more cities and towns that would be suitable for an American living abroad. Among the best of these are: Marbella, Torremolinos and Malaga, on the Southern Coast and Tossa de Mar, Cadaques, San Feliu de Guixols, Rosas, Tamariu, Playa de Aro and Ampurias, on the Costa Brava, north of Barcelona. On the Atlantic in the south both Cadiz and Huelva (from whence Colum¬bus sailed) are attractive but have comparatively small Anglo-American colonies. As a contrast, American military bases have recently been built in the Seville and Jerez (from whence comes Sherry) area and there are swarms of Americans. This ups your chances for employment or for starting a small business, but it also ups prices. On Majorca, the particularly recommended towns are Palma itself, the capital, and Deya, Soller, Formentor and Pollensa.

Of all these—and there are many more in Spain—I will choose two as examples, Torremolinos and Soller.

Torremolinos, just a short time ago was an unknown fishing village nestled up against a cliff. It had scenic beauty, miles of beaches in both directions, and had a quaint Spanish charm which brought its first foreigners—artists. Art colonies, as I've pointed out in the chapter devoted to them, grow slow at first, then at a rapidly accelerating speed. One artist tells another. Here is a beautiful, inexpensive, untouched, unsophisticated paradise. Soon writers, musicians, sculptors drift into town and following them, would-be artists and writers. As the colony grows retired folk with an interest in the arts begin finding homes, buying them, improving them. An American bar springs up, an American store, an American restaurant. And then, overnight, there are thousands of foreigners in town.

And thus it was with Torremolinos. Today she still retains her beauty, her climate, and most of her economy of living, but the untouched, unsophisticated qualities is gone. A paradise she remains, and probably one of the best spots in Spain in which to retire at any age.

Soller is in contrast to Torremolinos. Not nearly as overrun with tourists and short time sojourners, she is quieter, and cheaper than the southern city. About ten miles from Palma as the crow flies,

Soller is on the north coast of Majorca often described as the most beautiful coastline in the world. Actually, there are two towns, Soller proper and Puerta de Soller, the town's port which is about three miles away and nestled about a bay which has been used as a port since Phoenecian times. (In fact, skin divers are continually bringing up old wine and olive oil vases from Greek and Phoenecian times). A small trolley connects the two towns.

Swimming in Soller is superb with some of the clearest blue water this writer has ever seen this side of the South Pacific atolls. Such sports as skin diving reach their heights and boating is popular. Water sports are practical about nine months of the year, sometimes as many as eleven. Although on the water, Soller lays claim also to unrivaled mountain scenery since she is located in a small valley from which the tallest mountains on the island are seen to loom in all directions.

For the American on the lookout for a job, an investment, or interested in opening a business Torremolinos would be the better of these two cities, but a person primarily interested in retiring in a beautiful location and rock bottom prices would find Soller preferable. The number of Anglo-Americans is much smaller in Soller but those that do reside in this bargain paradise are more apt to be permanent. The "case histories" described below could in many cases be applied to either town. In fact, most of them could be applied to any of the dozen or more towns and villages enumerated above.

CHAPTER 10: THE ROMANCE OF FRANCE

In a nutshell. France is one of the largest nations in Europe both in area and in population with 213,009 square miles.

For probably the majority of Americans, France is the country that first comes to mind when retiring abroad is mentioned. This for many reasons but chief among them is the wide range of offerings France makes to the person wishing the good things of life. Scenically and climatically France rivals or surpasses her neighbors and she is the admitted cultural leader of the world. Paris, her capital, is so widely known and loved that it would be redundant to describe the "City of Light" here. The French Riviera, the Cote d'Azur, probably boasts more retired foreigners than any equal area in the world—and for good reason, of course.

But another cause for so many of us thinking in terms of France when we contemplate retiring abroad is because in the past France was one of the very cheapest countries in Europe. Back in the "seventies" and the "eighties" it was indeed quite possible to live in France, even in Paris, in comparative luxury and there were tens of thousands of Americans doing it.

Such a reputation did France build between the two World Wars as a land where one could retire on a shoestring, that the memory continues in people's minds until this day, in spite of the fact that it costs 25 times as much to live in Paris now as it did in the 30's. Twenty-five times as much!

Paris is, of course, considerably higher than the balance of the country but still the prospective American wishing to escape the work-a-day world should think twice before picking France as his home. That is, of course, unless he has a few gushers bringing him in an income. It is possible to retire in Paris but I am of the opinion that there are easier places in which to accomplish this end.

If you do find it possible to pick France as a country in which to retire, then you'll find what good life can really be. No place on earth do people eat and drink well than in France, absolutely no place. No city in the world can boast the cultural qualities of Paris. No place has the electric air, the vim, the love of life that Paris breaths. It is no mistake that she is called the City of Light.

And no country in the world exceeds France in the rich beauty of her provinces. Name a few of them over to yourself, the very pronouncing of them brings a feeling of glamour. Burgundy, Normandy, Brittany, Champagne, Gascony, Alsace and Lorraine.

THE FRENCH. There are two ways of melting the French.

If you're a tourist, dashing through the country, you'll probably wind up hating these people. The only ones you'll meet are hotel and restaurant employees, shop keepers and taxi cab drivers and these, of course, make their living by milking the tourist. You'll be no exception. Everywhere you go you'll meet the outstretched hand, no country is more tip hungry than France. And everywhere you go you'll probably feel you're being gypped and part of the time you'll be right. And even though you are a gregarious type person, interested in people and the way of life of others, you'll find the French home closed to you. You won't even meet any of the French, with the exception of those who wait on you.

But if you settle down in France, take a house or apartment, learn the language, than you will find another people. The Frenchman who has had the tourist pouring over the boundaries of his country for centuries has built up a barrier to them. He suffers them, because he must since France's largest single industry is tourism. But he keeps them at a distance so far as his personal life is concerned. He is another man when you settle more permanently.

The French as a people probably take more trouble to achieve the good life than any other in the world. Unless pushed by poverty, they wouldn't dream of eating poor food, wouldn't dream of sleeping in less than a comfortable bed, and wouldn't dream of not looking the best in regards to clothing. It has been no mistake that France has become the luxury nation of the world.

Once you have made friends of a French family, you will find them honest and hospitable, very good friends but very bad enemies. You'll find they have as great a love of country as any nation in the world and an attitude, even stronger than we Americans have about the States, that there just is no other place to live in the world but France.

MONEY. The French franc is one of the most fouled up currencies on earth. Not even the French trust it and when a Frenchman accumulates a bit of money he is more apt to buy gold with it and bury the metal under the floor than he is to put it in the bank.

One warning in changing dollars into francs. If you run short of francs, dealing with the black market (the noir, they call it) is risky. Particularly in Paris, the changers who hang around the vicinity of the American Express office are a vicious gang that will try every trick in the book from short changing you to slipping a few counterfeit bills in with the good ones. In fact don't follow one of these gentlemen down a dark alley to do your business transactions. If you do, there's a good chance that you won't come out again. If you do change any money on the black market in Paris, take along a French friend and preferably deal with someone he knows.

PRICES. As we've already pointed out above, prices in France are astronomical. They are the highest in Europe and for the average American it is probably more expensive to live in Paris than it is in New York. The average Frenchman might be another thing, but invariably the American is charged higher prices and he just doesn't know the ropes.

The same situation would probably apply if you took the Frenchman to America. Not that he would be deliberately overcharged in our country but he wouldn't know the ropes, wouldn't know where or how to find cheap rooms and the more economical restaurants. Wouldn't know what foods to buy, what shops to frequent.

PARTICULARLY RECOMMENDED LOCALITIES. I've been up and down and across France on various occasions and for varying lengths of time and strongly subscribe to the oft stated comment that all sections of France are desirable places in which to live and that it is a matter of personal preference. My own preferences are Paris and the Cote d'Azur.

Paris is a city that everyone should at least visit and preferably live in for a time, at least once in his life. You can find something favorable to say about almost any large city, but there is no other city which receives the acclaim honoring Paris.

The Riviera stretches from Marseilles to the Italian border, about a hundred-and-twenty miles by road. Nice is the capital but for many reasons not necessarily the most desirable town in which to live. For one thing the beach is so pebbly that it is almost impossible to walk barefooted down to the water. Besides, in my own opinion it's too large a city for this portion of the world. The Riviera, it has always seemed to me, should be devoted to small, clean, bright towns—not cities.

Cannes is the next largest town and with its excellent harbor is usually loaded with yachts and even the big liners from New York stop here to disgorge vacationers. For me a bit too expensive and still a bit too large.

There are a score of smaller towns and villages, each with their own attractions from Cassis near Marseille to Menton right on the Italian border. I particularly recommend the following as suited for man, woman or family retiring on a budget. Cassis, La Ciotat, Le Lavandou, St. Tropez, Boulouris, Cros de Cagnes, St. Paul, Beaulieu, Eze, Monte Carlo and Menton. There are many others.

Of them all, I believe I like Monte Carlo, largest town of the three towns in tiny Monaco, the land of Prince Rainer and Princess Grace. It has a charm all its own, this country which is smaller than 400 acres—an average size farm in the States.

It has been said that Monaco is a country nestled behind a billboard on the road between Nice and the Italian border and that when you pass through it by train you have to look sharp if you want to see it at all. And while all this may be true, surely she is tiny, little Monaco packs a charm into her small limits to be found nowhere else in Europe.

And actually she is probably a touch cheaper that the other sections of the Cote d'Azur, this because she is free of various taxes which France levels on her own citizens. Lower taxes mean cheaper prices and Monaco benefits in this wise.

There are other advantages for the person retiring on a shoestring and particularly one who is retiring without even the shoestring since Monaco has less of the restrictions that France puts on the foreigner residing within her borders. There is no military service, no income or property tax, and facilities for starting up a business without formalities of license are enjoyed.

Undoubtedly these freedoms are to be numbered among the reasons that Monaco actually has as permanent residents more foreigners than Monegasques.

Chapter 11: Italy the Eternal City

IN A NUTSHELL. The Republic of Italy is approximately the size of Arizona and if her population continues to grow at its present rate, will soon have the largest number of citizens of any European country save only the Soviet Union.

To give a quick rundown on Italy is a task beyond the meager abilities of this writer for there is probably no land in the world about which so very much can be said. To describe her geographically alone would take up pages since Italy runs from the Alps, the grandest mountains in Europe, down to the tropical-like Italian Riviera with its palm trees and its long golden beaches. Its northern industrial cities such as Milan are as modern as Detroit, while the sleepy villages in Southern Italy and Sicily are some of the most backward and poverty stricken in Europe. Such islands as Capri, right off Naples, have been noted since Roman times as resort spots and it was here that the notorious Emperor Tiberius built his retirement palace. Vesuvius, also near Naples, is probably the most famous volcano in the world—what school child doesn't remember Pompei and how it was destroyed over night by the belching mountain? Sicily, studded with Greek and Roman ruins, is considered by many travelers to have the most impressive coastline in Europe.

And her cities! If you were to name the dozen most beautiful cities in the world, Italy alone would boast at least two of them and possibly three. Venice, of course, with her canals, her medieval atmosphere, her different qualities; Rome, probably the most impressive city anywhere, with the weight of her centuries heavy on her shoulders; Florence, that medieval center which contains more of the great art of all time than any other city on earth.

Nor are these three alone. Naples has one of the most beautiful natural harbors in the world; Portofino, has one of the most beautiful natural settings anywhere; Positano, on the Amalfi Drive, south of Naples, is the loveliest art colony I have seen; San Remo on the Italian Riviera rivals anything on the French, including casinos, race tracks, luxury hotels and outstanding restaurants. There are many, many others.

Somehow, of all the countries in the world Italy packs more feeling of art and of history into her atmosphere. Not an hour goes by but that you are conscious of her heritage. Here is a Roman temple once built to Jupiter; there is a medieval castle rich with the wealth of the Medeci; over here is a cathedral ornamented by Michelangelo; the road over which we drive in spots still shows the ruts once caused by chariot wheels. Here Caesar passed on his way to Rome; there Napoleon was exiled on the tiny island of Elba; and from this house Marco Polo, the first tourist, took off on his way to far Cathay; and from this port the Crusaders left to wrest the Holy Land from Saladin.

There is no more attractive nation in the world than Italy. Were it not for one thing, I would recommend it to the skies for the American bent on retiring. The one thing is this: next to France, Italy is probably the most expensive country in Europe. And with her two million unemployed, it is one of the most difficult nations abroad in which to find work. It can be done, of course, and many Americans are living in Italy either retired on pensions or incomes or working at this deal or that. It can be done but there are easier places in which to retire than Italy.

THE ITALIANS. Somehow or other many of we Americans have picked up the idea that all Italians are short, dark of complexion, highly excitable, of criminal tendency and make second rate citizens. Why this should be, I don't know, unless it is because a large percentage of Italians who have migrated to the United States came from poverty stricken Sicily or from the equally poverty stricken areas about Naples.

Actually, Italy is almost as great a melting pot of nations as is our own country. There are a good many tall blondes in the north in those sections over which the Germanic tribes rolled to overthrow the Roman power. There are a great many red heads in the more central Rome area, and, in the deep-south we find the shorter statured, dark complicated Italians.

As far as criminal tendencies are concerned, it is true that Naples to a large extent deserves the reputation she has gained. There is probably more crime there than in the average European city. On the other hand, in the northern cities you are less apt to have your pockets picked, to be attacked on the streets, or to be cheated in your business dealings than you are in an average American city. I'd much sooner walk the streets of Venice, at two o'clock in the morning, than I would those of Brooklyn or Chicago.

The fabulous heights reached by the Italian people in art, science, political science and philosophy could not have been achieved by other than a bright, cultured, aggressive folk and not by a bunch of beetle-browed fruit peddlers such as are so often portrayed in our cartoons of typical Italians.

If you do choose Italy in which to sojourn, whether permanently or temporarily, you'll probably like the Italians, their food and drink, their outlook—their way of life. I certainly do.

MONEY. Not too many years ago Italian money was one of the weakest in Europe but today it is quite hard and you gain little by changing your dollars at the exchange houses.

Italian money, like French, can offer its hazards. The larger the bill the larger the size until when you get to the 10,000 lire notes you've got a piece of money that seems half the size of a baby blanket, and you have to fold it several times to get it into your wallet.

PRICES. We've mentioned elsewhere in this book that you can live cheaply just about anywhere if you know the ropes, even in Paris or New York.

PARTICULARLY RECOMMENDED LOCALITIES. If you go to Italy with the intention of finding some manner of making your own way, I would suggest Rome or possibly Venice. Both are large tourist centers, both have a good many Americans already living there. There are almost always opportunities when there are numbers of your fellows about. Rome in particular has at any one time several thousand Americans within her bounds, working, studying, conducting business or just plain retired. She is an alive, an inspiring city; it would be difficult to live in Rome and ever feel bored, ever feel as though life was an inescapable rut.

But for retiring on pension or income, or for a slower way of life, for me it would either be the Italian Riviera or Sicily. One great advantage in the former is its comparative accessibility to the balance of Europe. You might settle in a town such as Levanto and periodically make trips to nearby Switzerland, France, Monaco or even Yugoslavia, all of them less than a day's trip by car, bus or train.

Generally on the Italian Riviera the more expensive tourist centers are near the French border. There are as many picturesque and beautiful towns along here as there are on the French side. But if you are looking for economy, your best bet is to the East of Genoa, which for some reason has not as yet drawn the tourist hordes that other sections of the country are deluged with. In particular is the section around La Spezia. Of all the little towns in this stretch of the Italian Riviera, Monterosso and Levanto are my two favorites. But you have a wide variety and you might decide upon a little fishing village or some tiny town built up against the hillsides overlooking the blueness of the Mediterranean.

Sicily is, of course, the island just off the toe of the boot of Italy. Less than a mile of water separates her from the mainland. Messina is the town at which your ferry stops. When we think of Italy we think of Rome but actually Sicily was a Greek island, long before Rome became prominent. In fact, Syracuse was once the largest of all Greek cities, even surpassing Athens. Today, Greek theatres and temples are everywhere to be seen in their ruin.

Sicily has been "discovered" by the foreigner looking for bargain paradise retirement centers but she is a large island of 9,925 square miles, about the size of Maryland, and has a population of four and a half millions. There are literally hundreds of towns, cities and villages beautifully situated that are as yet untouched by the outsider.

My own favorite Sicilian town is Taormina and I once spent an extremely happy time there. The famous Mt. Etna, snow topped, is in the distance and Taormina herself is built atop a high cliff which rises almost perpendicularly out of the sea. There is a famous Greek-Roman theatre and other historic ruins since the city has been in existence for some three thousand years. There are also medieval ruins and in fact the whole city with its picturesque winding streets and its walls and gates, gives you a middle-ages effect.

Taormina has been well "discovered" and particularly in season becomes quite crowded with tourists. However, a permanent resident can beat tourist prices by having his own house or apartment and shopping in the markets as the Italians do, rather than eating in restaurants.

I know of only two places in Europe that boast a better climate, the Greek Dodecanese Islands and the Costa del Sol of southern Spain.

CHAPTER 12: THE CHARM OF AUSTRIA

IN A NUTSHELL. Once proud Austria, largest of European Empires, now has a land area of but 32,375 square miles and a population of about seventeen million. She compares with Maine or Indiana in size and her total population is less than that of New York City.

But although the Austro-Hungarian Empire is no longer the gigantic hodge-podge of nations it once was, Austria herself still lives and there is a unique feeling, in this little land, of glories of the past that never leaves you.

Vienna, for instance, once the capital of the empire, still retains the charms of yesteryear and there are few cities in the world more charming, more beautiful, and more gay. And Vienna, despite the smallness of the country today is the 22nd largest city in the world with a population pushing two million. It is the great metropolis of Central Europe.

But Vienna isn't Austria, no matter how proud the Austrians may be of their capital. Austria, despite size, packs a great deal of wallop into her countryside. In the western provinces such as Vorarlberg and the Tyrol, we have Alpine grandeur equal to that of Switzerland, and the winter sports enthusiasts are as keen about this area as they are any place in the world. Salzburg, on the German border, noted for its music festivals and as the birthplace of Mozart, is proclaimed by many to be the most beautiful example of Germanic medieval city remaining in Europe. And Innsbruck, another age-old town, is in the most striking mountain setting I have ever seen.

But listing interesting and lovely Austrian cities could take several pages and we have space limitation. We should also touch on the Austrian countryside, because if the Austrians themselves are to be considered judges of the outstanding qualities of their land, it is the countryside that is above all appealing. I have never seen a people so prone to take off at the least sign of a gleam of sunshine and go hiking, driving, picnicking, bicycling, canoeing, and mountain climbing as the Austrians. I seriously estimate that at least one million people stream out of the city and head for the forests, rivers, mountains and fields. You've never seen anything like it. Hundreds of thousands of them will be wearing lederhosen (short leather pants) and carrying knapsacks on their backs.

They are a people devoted to the outdoors and there is no wonder in this since the Austrian outdoors are surpassed nowhere. I believe that one of the strongest memories I shall always have was a picnic I went on with an Austrian couple one unblemished July day. We drove from Vienna to Mariazell, a small town to which yearly is made pilgrimages. Nearby a towering mountain's peak can be reached by a cable-lift (a startling experience in itself). On the very top we spread our lunch and ate and drank our Gumpoldskirchner wine, while looking out over what must have been the greater part of Austria.

This book is by no means a travel guide, but in dealing with Austria I must certainly mention the fact that if you are a good food fan, then Austria is a land you will love and Vienna a city you will adore. Austrian restaurant prices are a fraction of those of France or Italy and by the very cosmopolitan nature of Austria's capital, the variety of dishes is endless. The specialties of those lands once contained within the Austro-Hungarian Empire are also specialties of Austria so you can run the gamut from Germanic sausages to Italian pastas, from Hungarian goulash to Czech roast goose, or Yugoslav brodet. And I must add a personal note; as a beer drinker from way back, I have never found a beer I liked better than the Viennese Schwechater dunkle (dark).

If retirement on a shoestring is your desire, if you wish to find a beauty spot in which to settle down, permanently or semi-permanently, you have few better bets than Austria. If I were to list in order the cheapest countries in Europe it would probably go: Spain, Greece, Austria, Portugal, Ireland, and Norway. But if I had to list them by compatibility of the people it would be: Austria, Ireland, Norway, Spain, Greece, and Portugal. Because there is one important thing Austria has which the other economical countries haven't to nearly as great a degree. She has a people that you will get to know, who will be your equals (if not superiors) in education, culture and progressiveness. In short, you will love the Austrians. Everyone does.

There is just one word of warning. Personally, I like to follow the sun and I haven't spent a winter in a northern climate for some years. Summers, yes, winters, no. Austria is a country as famed for its winters as it is for its summers. If you like the change in season, wonderful. If you like winter weather, swell. But if you don't, stay out of Austria because she has winter and lots of it. The warm months are from the middle of May to the middle of September.

THE AUSTRIANS. Theoretically the Austrians are a branch of the Germans. The name of their country means "Eastern Germany." However, in spite of the fact that the language has no differences, Austrians and Germans are nearly as different as Greeks and Norwegians.

It's a matter of gemuetlichkeit. It's a matter of an easy going, kindly, friendly, gay approach to life. You find little grimness among the Austrians. They love life, nature, good food, good drink, good companionship. They're in no hurry, either to get rich or to get to whatever destination they might have at the time.

An Austrian from Vienna, in short, would drive a good Prussian resident of Berlin, stark raving; and vice versa.

Just one thing. Tipping. I have never seen such a tip-conscious people. Everybody tips everybody. I have a theory that in the old days, the Emperor used to tip the kings and princes under him. They in turn tipped the dukes, barons, counts (and no-accounts) under them. Who in turn tipped the businessmen and shopkeepers. Who in turn tipped the waiters, hotel employees and such. Who in turn tipped everyone with whom they dealt with. But whether or not this was the way it was in the old days that are the way it is today. Perhaps it all works out the same in the end for the Austrians. You tip and get tipped. At the end of the day you're even. But for a foreigner in the country all I can say is keep a big pocketful of change and don't forget such folk as streetcar conductors, the mail man, the shop girl, the service station attendant and the theatre usher.

Chapter 13: Historic Great Britain

In a Nutshell. Great Britain, including Northern Ireland, has a land area of but 94,212 square miles but a population of over 50 million. This means she is about the size of our Wyoming or Oregon but runs neck and neck with Western Germany in having the largest population in Europe save the Soviet Union.

It's been said over and over that the reason the British are the greatest colonizers the world has ever seen is because they have such a terrible climate that they flee abroad. And actually I'm not going to argue the point. The only place I've lived with so much rain is Portland, Oregon.

Be that as it may, England still has its gracious beauty. Largely manmade, but nature does her share too. So much rain could only result in a fabulously green and be flowered countryside, and so it is.

But in man-made sights, England cannot be surpassed. Her buildings go back to prehistory. The famed Stonehenge was built long centuries ago, before the coming of the Romans in 41 B.C. Roman ruins are here, there and the other place and such early Briton ones as Tintagel in Cornwall, reputedly the place where King Arthur was born. It was with the coming of the Normans in 1066 A.D. that the castles which are England's glory began to be erected. Today there are so many of these that the British Travel Association puts out a special booklet for tourists entitled Castles in Britain which lists 48 of the best preserved. With the discovery of the New World, England's empire began to grow and with it an enormous wealth was put into the cities, towns and villages of England. Cathedrals, palaces, government buildings, churches, fortresses—and the most picturesque pubs in the world. It would be hard, in Great Britain, to be able to get more than a mile or two away from some worthwhile sight.

London, until just recently, was the biggest city in the world and for long years had carried this distinction. Tokyo is now larger, in population, but in many respects London is still the most important city on earth. This is not because of the number of her inhabitants but due to the fact that through this great sprawling city for centuries the biggest Empire the world has even seen was governed. As a result the British museum is the greatest library in the world. St. Paul's possibly the greatest cathedral, The City is the greatest banking and commercial center of the world (with the possible exception of Wall Street) and Lloyd's of London which is in The City is the largest insurance network. We could go on adding to this list indefinitely but to what end? Everyone knows of the grandness of London.

In many respects, England is the ideal place for an American to retire. The language advantages are obvious and no country offers so much in the way of entertainment, cultural activities and opportunities to pursue a study of almost any subject as does England. Plays, movies, radio and TV must remain a mystery to us in France, Italy or Spain until we learn the language. But in England all these are immediately ours to enjoy.

Nor is England one of the expensive nations of Europe. London, unfortunately is high, particularly in rents, but otherwise England is one of the cheaper countries. Except for tobacco and alcoholic beverages which are taxed tremendously. In fact, the foreigner residing in England is even eligible for many of the socialized medicine advantages.

THE BRITISH. If you have in mind the classic cartoon character of an Englishman wearing a monocle, lacking in humor, and limiting his conversation to an occasional "By Jove"—forget about it. As far as physical appearance is concerned, the British look about the same as we do. Possibly they average a bit shorter in height. As far as a sense of humor is concerned, you'll find every type of humor in England, just as you will in our own land. And the one big advantage is that in England you can understand their jokes and they can understand yours.

You can find every type of Englishman, just as you can every type of American. Good, bad, indifferent. No, I take that back. There is one kind you'll never find; one that wears a monocle and says "By Jove."

The British people are good natured, hospitable, courteous, well disciplined, and averagely handsome. And eat absolutely the worst food in the civilized world.

MONEY. British money is the most incomprehensible on earth. Who dreamed up their money system I haven't the vaguest idea but it makes no more sense than their weights and measures. (The English "foot" which is also used in America, was decided upon because it was the length of the king's foot some centuries ago.)

Coins come in halfpenny, one penny, three pence, six pence, one shilling, two shillings, two shillings and six pence. And paper money comes in 10 shillings, one pound and five pound notes.

If the above doesn't confuse you, you'll find that many prices are listed in guineas which are worth a pound, one shilling. But there is no such coin or note as a guinea. They also call their two shilling six pence coin a Half Crown, but there is no such thing as a "Crown."

To top it off, all the coins are called by slang terms. A shilling is a "bob," a pound is a "quid," sixpence is a "tanner," two shillings is a Florin.

PRICES. London is one of the more expensive cities of Europe and Great Britain one of the cheapest countries.

In the country it is another thing. The more remote you get, the cheaper you will find cottages and houses.

Tobacco and alcoholic beverages are highly taxed and even more expensive than in the States with the exception of beer which is still, however, high by European standards. But food is considerably cheaper than at home and of excellent quality. One thing you'll probably like in England is the fact that frozen food is seen more than in any country except our own. Canned goods are also more widely used than in most European countries although they aren't as cheap as at home.

Things like movies and theatres are low priced, compared to the U.S. In general, clothing is cheaper than in our own country and of excellent quality.

PARTICULARLY RECOMMENDED LOCATIONS. I suppose that if from the first we hadn't decided upon absolute honesty in this book, I could read up on some of the travel guides and tourist literatures published by every country, and give you a second hand rundown on portions of England that I have never seen. But I'm not going to do that. I have gone by train and bus through a limited few sections of England, but actually I have never lived for any period of time in any location except London.

This wasn't due to any lack of curiosity on my part, nor a belief that the British countryside is less than attractive. It is simply that every time I go to England, with intentions of going into the interior, I get tied up in London which is a town I love. Something happens, and I never go beyond her city limits, or, at least, not very far beyond.

So I am going to limit this report to London as I find it.

I don't know about you, but personally I go on "kicks." That is I'll get onto some hobby, or some study, or some sport and ride it to death for a time. For instance, I once took a trip through Turkey and happened to see the Hittite museum in Ankara. I'd hardly heard about the Hittites before although I've always been an avid reader of history. Nothing would do but that I must go on a "Hittite kick." I went to the museums, I bought a few little Hittite seals and clay statues in the bazaars, and I read every book I could find on this early civilization. The kick lasted for a few months and then something else came up—mountain climbing, I think.

At any rate, London is probably the ideal city in the world to go on a "kick." I don't care what your interest is, London will be able to supply you with opportunity to study it, go into it, and enjoy it. There are the theatres, the museums, the libraries, the specialty stores, the clubs and associations, the societies, to afford you anything from a close up study of spiritualism to skin diving. And

I'm not exaggerating.

London, in short, has everything. The only other city I can think of that remotely approaches her is New York, but even New York fails in many respects to live up to London. It's true you can get just about anything, do just about anything in New York, if you have the money. In London, you can do it without a great deal of money. For instance, how would you like to foot the bill in New York for going to the current top ten theatre hits? Brother! But the last time I was in London I was able to accomplish this without strain at all.

Even though you had no intention of living permanently in London I would say that every member of the English speaking world should spend some time in this capital. For, actually, London is the capital not only of Great Britain and the Commonwealth of Nations, but is the cultural capital of English speaking people everywhere. At least that's my opinion and so I found her.

Chapter 14: The Islands of Greece

IN A NUTSHELL. Today Greece is one of the smaller and less important nations of Europe. Her size is approximately that of Alabama even counting all of her islands and her population less than New York's. In a way it is hard to believe that this is the land from which sprang Western Civilization.

Mainland Greece is not, largely, one of the more attractive countries of the continent. The greater part of her land area is mountainous, rocky and colorless. There are exceptions, of course, many of them.

It is in her coasts and her islands that Greece achieves beauty, and I doubt if I've ever taken a more exciting trip by sea than those inter-island journeys that leave Piraeus, the port of Athens, for the Cyclades, the Dodecanese, Crete, Lesbos, Corfu and the others. On such trips it is easily seen why the Greeks, or rather the Minoans who preceded them, became the first great seafarers. Each island of the Aegean Sea is within sight of two or three more at least. And they stretch like a bridge from the Asia Minor coast to the Greek mainland. Even primitive man must have been able to construct adequate craft to make such short journeys early in human history. In fact, remains are found on the larger islands of the Neolithic period.

Greece, at the height of her Golden Age achieved pinnacles that many scholars consider never to have been passed since. The Parthenon on the Acropolis is named the most perfect building ever constructed. The greatest philosophers the world has known walked the streets of Athens hundreds of years before the birth of Christ. The sciences, our modern law, the theatre, literature, all had either their beginnings or tremendous impetus from this poor land.

Today she is largely a sad memory. Everywhere you see the remains of the Old Greece, the temples, the walls, the theatres, the sad fallen columns. And it is in this Old Greece that you find the land's appeal, for modern Greece is one of the most poverty stricken and backward countries of Europe. Only in Spain, Portugal and Yugoslavia do you see the poverty that you find in Greece.

As always when wages are low and the people poor, the country is a cheap place in which to reside. Greece is today, possibly the cheapest country in Europe, the only possible rival being Spain, another land of poverty and low wages. As always, the larger cities such as Athens and Salonika are higher priced but even Athens is cheap compared to any other capital of Europe.

I would say that to retire in Greece, either on a small income or with the intention of working out some local manner of making a living, you should have a basic interest in the cultural background of the country, otherwise you might find life in Greece on the drab and uninteresting side, particularly if you remained in Athens or elsewhere on the mainland.

THE GREEKS. The Greeks will tell you that everyone in Greece would like to immigrate to the United States, including the king. And they aren't joking. I doubt that there is a family in Greece that doesn't have more than one close relative in the United States. It is a regular tradition with them to go to America, make their fortunes, and possibly even take out citizenship and then to return to their own country in their old age to live out their lives. A fortune to a Greek can be pretty small potatoes since even a Social Security pension is a lot of money in Greece. I knew quite a few women in Rhodes whose husbands had gone to the United States figuring on staying twenty or thirty years and then returning. The wives were patiently sitting out the time. Each month a check would come from America to keep them and the children.

With all this it becomes obvious that America and Americans are well known and well liked by the Greeks. A great deal of English is spoken and you have no difficulty in making your wants known. This is one country in which it seems almost impossible to learn even the few words needed for shopping and the conduct of everyday life, but it's not too necessary to attempt to learn Greek since so many of the people speak your language.

MONEY. Only a few years ago Greece had one of the weakest currencies in Europe and finally the drachma fell to the point where it took 30,000 to make one dollar. However, Uncle Sam came to the rescue and backed the Greek currency. The Greek government, to simplify things, merely lopped off the last three zeros in 1984 and the money has remained firm ever since. There is little if any advantage in bringing free market money into Greece. You might as well change your dollars at the bank or at your hotel.

PRICES. As I have already said above, prices are probably as cheap as anywhere in Europe. Prices will vary considerably between Athens and the other large cities and the small islands seldom touched by foreigners.

On the island of Rhodes there are no import taxes, the result of a government measure to attract tourists and consequently there are some unbelievable bargains. This same lack of tax results in German cameras selling for less than they do in Germany, French perfumes for less than in France, Swiss watches for less than in Switzerland. German, Danish, Dutch and Czech beers, the best in the world, sell for a third of what they cost in Scotland.

PARTICULARLY RECOMMENDED LOCALITIES. I can't recommend the mainland at all, and of the islands I really know well only Rhodes and Corfu.

In some respects Corfu has its advantages over Rhodes as a retirement spot. For one thing it is only a short ferry hop, a mile or so, from the mainland, while Rhodes is an overnight trip by inter-island boat. And Corfu is also handy in that it is easily available to Italy. An overnight trip takes you to Brindisi and from there you are in Naples or Rome in a matter of hours. Corfu has a large foreign colony too, particularly retired English, while the foreign colony of Rhodes is largely limited to the permanently based American servicemen there. The swimming, the scenery, the prices on Corfu, we have no arguments about. It is a charming, pleasant island on which to consider retirement.

However, the town of Rhodes, on the island of Rhodes, is the most beautiful city in the world.

I have done a good deal of traveling in the past decade and can state that of all cities these I think the most beautiful: Mexico City, Paris, Rome, Venice, New Orleans, San Francisco, Istanbul and Tangier (not necessarily in that order). But Rhodes is the most beautiful city in the world.

In the days of the Trojan War there were three Greek towns on the island and they supplied ships to join Agamemnon's expedition against Troy, but in the year 408 B.C. they decided to unite and form one big town which they named Rhodes. Later the city fell to the Romans and later the Byzantines took over. But in 1308 the Knights of St. John, a Crusader order, captured the island and it was they who built the city we see today.

Rhodes is a medieval city. The walls which still surround it are in good enough condition to withhold a siege right now. It's streets are still cobblestoned, the shops where you buy bread, wine and olive oil for your daily needs are the same shops that dealt in the same commodities 600 years ago. The little taberna where you stop to have a glass of beer or retsina wine once served knights in armor.

Rhodes means Roses and indeed this is an island of flowers. The parks that surround the moats of the fortress walls are abloom with flowers all year around and are particularly heavily splashed with reds.

I believe that I've already stated in this book that there is no place in Europe that equals the climate of Florida or even southern California. There is no other place where you can swim all year round. The nearest to it is achieved on the Costa del Sol of Spain and in the Dodecanese Islands of which Rhodes is the capital. In Rhodes we found the best climate in Europe.

When the United States began spotting broadcast stations about the world to pipe our propaganda into the communist and Near East countries, Rhodes was one of the chosen locations. Here is permanently stationed the U.S. Coast Guard Cutter, the Courier. And on it are more than one hundred American servicemen.

The coming of the Courier brought big changes to Rhodes which ordinarily has a population of 128,000. Some forty of the servicemen brought their families but that was just the beginning. Various civilians connected with the Voice of America, also showed up. Teachers for the American school, and doctors and dentists of Greek-American extraction. Uncle Sam paid the way for the service men bringing over their cars, refrigerators and other American needs.

Greek houses were not up to American standards, so new houses were built, and this amounted to a regular little building boom since most of the local population was dwelling in houses erected five hundred years ago. The shop-keepers put in new products they'd never heard of before to meet new demands. News shops opened carrying American newspapers and magazines.

The American money was a boom to the Greeks and it also works out well for a civilian American living on Rhodes. The presence of these State-side comforts, many of which are not to be found in other sections of Greece, makes living that much the easier.

And there's another angle. The service families are periodically rotated and seldom do they take back home all the refrigerators, stoves and what-not gadgets that they brought out with them. Instead they are sold locally for whatever they will bring and I will estimate that there is no place else outside of the United States where American household appliances are so economically priced, second hand.

I think the little city of Rhodes is one of the top places in the world for retirement. There is just one limitation which is a serious one for such gregarious persons as myself. Your companionship is largely limited to the service families from the Courier most of whom are quite young, few of whom have much in the way of education. There are some wonderful exceptions, but let's face it, on the average the professional serviceman isn't the best company in the world.

Chapter 15: The Kingdom of Morocco

IN A NUTSHELL. Morocco is both old-old and still one of the most recent additions to the family of nations. A bit larger than California in size and with roughly ten million persons, until 1956 Morocco was a French protectorate. This protectorate had been imposed on the Moroccans in 1912 at which time the international powers were gleefully splitting up what little remained of the world not already assimilated. The Spanish took over the northern 7,589 square miles of the country and the French the rest.

But in spite of the fact that the average Moroccan is poorly educated in matters economic and political they do know one thing. If they want to put up with misrule they want it to be Moors who are misruling them, not foreigners.

I had the interesting experience of living in Morocco at the time of their successful revolt against the French and Spanish. I watched the parades in the streets, watched the French and Spanish foreign legions try to quell the rioting Moors, who, using him as a symbol, were demanding return of their sultan who had been exiled by the French. I even met various of the gun-runners who were supplying the guerrillas in the interior with arms to battle the hapless French troops.

The French finally called it quits and today Morocco is tranquil again. And like all nations she is eyeing tourism with a gleam of avarice. This source of income, Morocco would love to tap. She is making a great push to attract American and other tourists to her sights, and indeed she should be successful.

Morocco is handy to the tourist and offers a great deal that is truly different. The majority of tourists, American as well as European, are not in the money bracket to take long trips to the Near or Far East but Morocco offers much the same as you find in those far countries Iraq, Iran, Jordan and Turkey. European countries aren't actually too very different from our own. European

Cities, largely, look a great deal like American ones and Europeans dress, eat and conduct themselves much the same as we Americans do. But Morocco is truly different.

I would be very much surprised if Morocco's attempts to get the tourist trade in large numbers failed. I expect the country to have a tourist boom and not only that but to attract large numbers of foreign residents. She has scenic beauty, picturesque and attractive cities, excellent sports facilities, wonderful business opportunities, excellent climate, and is as cheap as Spain.

THE MOORS. Actually you will not get to know many native Moroccans, even though you permanently retire in Morocco. You are more apt to associate with other foreigners principally French and Spanish although there are quite a few Americans and British, especially in Tangier. Few Moroccans speak English and few indeed are educated at all. In spite of its position on the Atlantic coast, Morocco is an Eastern Land and in many respects is more backward than Turkey and the other Near Eastern Moslem countries.

Those Moslems that you do meet, the few who speak English, you will probably like; they make good friends. These, by the way, will all be men. You won't meet Moslem women. For all practical purposes, the Moorish women are still in the days of the harem.

Although there is some movement, sparked by one of the royal princesses, to modernize woman's position, the greater number goes veiled in the streets.

There is, of course, no reason to fear the Moroccan. He is probably less criminally inclined that the average American. As I think back, I cannot recall ever having met a Moor that I disliked.

MONEY. Once upon a time, the French franc and the Spanish peseta were the currencies most widely used in Morocco. Now, however, these have been withdrawn and the Moroccan franc has taken over.

When you speak of money in Morocco then you must consider Tangier, once, and possibly still, the greatest international money clearing center of the world.

The capitalist system is a complicated one and nowhere does it become more complicated than in the field of international finance. There is not a nation in the world, including our own, that hasn't passed some truly gobbledygook laws in an attempt to strengthen its own currency to the detriment of the others of the world.

To bring a balance to things at all, it became necessary to establish clearing houses where the world's currencies found their true level, no matter what laws might be passed at home. Tangier became one of these clearing houses, Switzerland another. And in these two places you may buy, or sell, any currency, or gold, at its true value.

Not even in the United States can you legally buy gold coins or bullion, but you can in Tangier at any bank. If you mistrust your country's currency, you can sink your savings into gold, keeping them safe from inflation. There are something like fifty banks in this small city, and uncounted hordes of private money changers.

PARTICULARLY RECOMMENDED LOCALITY. Although I spent six or seven months in Morocco at one time and have visited it for short periods on half a dozen occasions, the only area I really know is Tangier. I have traveled across the country north and south and east and west, but not to the point where I could advise on permanent location. Consequently I'll deal with Tangier alone.

The town's name was Tingis originally and was founded by the Phoenicians about 1600 B.C. Phoenician, Carthaginian, Greek and Roman ruins are to be seen in the vicinity and there is a small local museum which houses some of the objects found in or near Tangier from ancient times. Since then the city has been held by Byzan¬tines, Vandals, Visigoths and finally the Arabs. In more modern times it has been taken and held for varying periods by the Portuguese, English and Spanish and for a time an International Commission of eight countries. All of these races have made their imprints on the city.

Some of the world's most beautiful cities owe a considerable portion of their attractiveness to their geographical location, such as Rio de Janeiro, Naples, Sydney, San Francisco. And such is

Tangier. Like most ancient cities she is perched atop a hill and her early fortifications surrounded what is now the medina. The Sultan's palace is at the very top of the hill, the casbah section, and from here you can look out over the Atlantic, the Mediterranean and the Straits of Hercules. Through these straits, one of the busiest waterways in the world, you can usually see a dozen ships or so at any one time. Far to the south are the imposing Atlas Mountains where once, supposedly, Hercules held up the weight of the heavens.

Tangier has one feature which is quite wonderful. In most cities of the Near East and the Far East you will find extreme picturesque qualities but from time to time, if you reside in one, you have periods where you wish for the sight of broad boulevards, numerous cars, neon signs, big movie houses, huge department stores—and a malted milk and grilled cheese sandwich. You long for these things—but don't get them. In Tangier, you can realize every one. Tangier is one of the most modern cities across the waters. At least the European section is. You can be deep in the cool darkness of the streets of the Casbah, flavoring the atmosphere of the Arab world. Then, if you wish, you can walk in five minutes to what you would think a modern California or Florida town. Modern cars will honk at you, fashionably dressed women will parade by hauling their clipped poodles behind them. Neon lights will blink at you, and if you wish, tune in your radio to the American radio stations which broadcast from Tangier to all Europe, the Voice of America and various other projects. There is an American school, if you have children, and an American club if you like swimming and golfing with your fellow Americans.

If you like sport, keep in mind that Tangier has what is sometimes called the third best beach in the world. There is a yacht club, a Polo ground, tennis courts, horse racing, air and motor rallies, hunting and fishing, hiking and skiing (in the nearby Atlas mountains). In short, this section of Morocco can supply just about any sport in which you might be interested. There is even a bullring and the biggest matadors of Spain fight here each year.

The foreign colony is an extensive one and you can find just about any type of person you wish in Tangier. There are many American families living permanently in town, working for the Voice of America, for the Legation, for branches of American business houses. These live a rather conservative life, centered largely around their own American club. They are inclined to buy a great deal of their daily needs through the American P-X, and keep largely from contact with other members of the European colony.

To the other extreme is the Bohemian set which hangs out largely in Dean's internationally famous bar, at the Safari and at the Parade. Dean's is run by an Egyptian educated in London and is known by every international celebrity in the world. But the Parade and the Safari are American owned and operated and the most popular hangouts for American writers, artists, movie people and such—not to speak of plain out and out bums of the alimony-from-home variety.

It between these two groups is a good many Americans, British and other English speaking elements. You'd be able to find your own level, in Tangier. Barbara Hutton has one of her larger, and one of her best-liked homes right in the Casbah, so you'll see that all types of Americans are to be found here, not just those who retire on a shoestring.

Chapter 16: Japan, The Land of The Rising Sun

IN A NUTSHELL. Our word Japan comes from the Chinese zapagn which means to the east, or source of the sun. The Japanese call their country Nippon which means rising sun. Possibly no nation in the world has gone through such extremes of expansion and contraction as has Japan in the past century but today she has an area of 142,266 square miles and a population of about 85 million. This makes her a bit smaller than Montana but one of the most populous countries of the world being surpassed only by China, India, the U.S.S.R. and our own country.

Tokyo, the capital, is now the world's largest city passing both New York and London and she is still growing.

The Japanese Empire consists of four principal islands, Honshu, Hokkaido, Kyushu and Shikoku and roughly a thousand smaller ones. Even were her land mass largely arable she would still be crowded with that population but actually Japan, and this comes as a surprise to many Westerners, can cultivate only 20% of her land area which makes her people so concentrated that there are few places on earth with a greater density of population.

Stretching as she does almost due north and south for a thousand miles, Japan can offer a wide range of climate. The northern island of Hokkaido can be quite cold but Kyushu and the islands still further south are mild and warm. In fact, the climatic difference is compared to Maine at one extreme and Georgia to the other. Scenically she has much to offer, her famed mountains such as Fujiyama are as spectacular as any in the world, her short rapid rivers, her forests of pine, her sandy beaches, her long stretches of rice paddies, her lovely lakes. All of these you have seen portrayed on Japanese prints. Japan can boast a beautiful land but by no means is it all delicate in its beauty as some Westerners seem to believe.

Children in Japanese schools are still taught that the Nipponese people are of divine origin and that the Empire was first founded in 660 B.C. by the Emperor Jimmu who was a direct descendant of the sun-goddess. Be that as it may, modern Japanese history begins with an American fleet sailing into Japanese waters in 1854 to force the backward feudalistic country to open its ports to foreign trade. Commodore Perry didn't have any idea what he was starting when that was accomplished.

The Japanese, militarily unable to resist, capitulated in humiliation but in no time at all decided that the only way to resist was to end feudalism and establish capitalism. So rapidly did they assimilate western ideas and industrial techniques that by 1894 they were strong enough to fight a war with China and take over Formosa and the Pescadores Islands. And that was just the beginning. Russia at that time was considered a great world power, but in 1904 Japan took on the Czar's forces and trounced them, gaining a foothold in Manchuria. Korea was taken in 1910 and suddenly the western powers realized they had created a Frankenstein monster, which, far from being a market for their manufactured goods, was now competing with them. In less than sixty years from the time Perry's squadron of American ships had humbled Japan, the dynamic little country had become a world power.

We all know more recent history. The ruling class of Japan made its big bid in 1941—and failed. Occupation followed and some changes, surface changes in the governmental form. However, today Japan is once again one of the great powers of the world. Her textiles and other exports are flowing out of the country at a rate considerably greater than before the Second World War, and once again the mercantile nations of Europe and America are aghast at her competition.

Her merchant fleet, all but completely destroyed in the war, once again is to be seen in every port. I'll never forget standing on the bridge of a rusty Liberty ship, now floating the Dutch flag, and watching a Japanese freighter overtake and pass us, new, fast, and smart. The Dutch captain muttered to me, "Who won the war, anyway? We can't begin to compete with their shipping rates."

During the war years we Americans were subject to the usual war propaganda which gave us to understand that Japanese products were all shoddy and inferior and that the Japanese were capable only of copying the developments of the more intelligent nations (such as ourselves, of course). However, today there are probably few people who don't realize that when cameras such as the Nikon and Canon begin edging out the best products of Germany such as Leica and Contax, they are the product not of a nation of copy-cats but an intelligent, capable, aggressive people. Rapid changes are taking place in Japan, she has rebuilt the damage of the war years, and she is quietly but deliberately and efficiently slipping out from under the thumb of American domination and again setting her own path. She is a modern, progressive nation, warm with life and growth. It will be interesting to watch her developments in the next decade.

THE JAPANESE. When I was a young boy the family lived for a time in Southern California and it was there that I formed my first opinions of the Japanese. We lived in El Monte, a few miles out of Los Angeles proper and quite a few of our neighbors were Japanese making their livings on small farms. You couldn't have had better neighbors. They were quiet, courteous, thoughtful—and tolerant of us children, even though we did make a habit of raiding strawberry and melon patches. In school the half dozen or more Japanese children invariably took all the top honor roll positions and then when the bell rang went home and instead of playing worked for possibly six hours in the fields with their parents.

I was highly impressed by the California Japanese.

Nor will you find them basically different in Japan.

They are a polite, good natured, honest, hard working, intelligent, progressive, family loving, good food loving, and above all, cleanly people worthy of your respect.

Language will offer you few barriers if you sojourn or retire in Japan. English has become the international language of commerce and the Japanese teach it widely in their schools. It is probably more often studied than all the rest of the western languages put together.

Their way of life is, of course, considerably different from the American and European way. It must be remembered that within the memory of Japanese still alive this was a feudalistic country living under a social system that our own western countries have not known for centuries. However, many of the remnants of this in particular are far from unpleasant. Such things as the Kabuki which is classical drama going back several hundred years and consists of dancing and singing as well as acting. Such things as the Bon orori folk dancing. Such things as the kimono dress and geta clogs. Such things as the tea ceremony and Bunraku puppet shows, the dainty formal gardens, the endless numbers of temples and shrines, the characteristic art forms found nowhere else on earth.

MONEY. One hundred sen make a yen, the symbol of which is Y. The currency is fairly strong.

PRICES. There is one thing that must be understood in living abroad, whether it be Europe, Mexico, Africa—or Japan. If you are seeking to live economically, then you must learn to live the way the people of the country do. To live the way an American does, be it in New York or Rolla, Missouri, is out of the question abroad if you are on a budget.

Nowhere does this apply more than it does to the oriental countries and the reason should be obvious. To export the American way of life half way around the world costs money. Their way of life is geared to their local economy and it is considerably easier and certainly cheaper for you to adapt to their way than to try and get them to adjust to yours.

You will meet people who will tell you that living in Japan are terribly expensive. And you will meet others who will tell you that you can live wonderfully well on a comparative pittance.

Both are right.

If you find it impossible to adjust to the Japanese way of life but insist on eating, dressing and entertaining yourself in American fashion and living in an American type hotel or house, it will cost you plenty. But if you eat Japanese food, drink Japanese beverages, enjoy Japanese entertainment forms and live in a Japanese type house, you can do it on surprisingly little.

Chapter 17: How to Begin the Journey

As I pointed out in the chapter entitled When Do You Plan to Retire?, the reader who is seriously determined to get out of the rat-race and build a new and satisfactory life in retirement, must decide to do it now.

If you lack this determination to do it now, you will probably never do it at all and retirement will come to you, if it ever comes, at the age of 65 or more when most of life has passed you by.

But if you have read this far in this book and have assimilated what I've had to say, you should have that determination.

To do it now!

However, I have no desire to send you off half-cocked. We want to do it now but we also want to do it right. We want to go into this cool minded, determined, and using every advantage we can find to assure ourselves of success. Tens of thousands of others have done it. People who were no more intelligent and with no more of the "breaks" on their side than you have on yours. "Breaks" are made, there is no such thing in reality as "luck."

Fine. What is the first step?

I divide the readers of this book into three groups, roughly.

The first group is that person, or family, that has a pension or income which they have thus far thought of as insufficient upon which to retire.

The second group is that of a person, or family, which has a very small income which truly is not enough upon which to retire, at least not on a desirable scale.

The third group, is that of a person or family that has no regular income at all—but still wishes to retire.

Let's take them one by one.

GROUP No. 1. Let us say you have a regular monthly income. I have no idea what the source may be. It might be a pension, military or otherwise, or it might be social security or even investments in stocks, bonds or what have you.

You can retire on this income and live a full existence without ever doing another lick of work in your life. But you cannot do it on a keeping-up-with-the-Joneses basis. And probably you can't do it in your present locale, since the majority of Americans today live in the big cities or in their vicinities and this is exactly where prices are such as to be prohibitive.

Your first step, then, is thoroughly to investigate those places both in our own country and abroad where you can live on such an amount.

In this book we have already indicated a good many foreign countries and American bargain paradises and art colonies. Probably the descriptions of one or more have interested you.

The job now, then, is to investigate these further. Go all out, to find everything you can about those localities. Do not go off without further investigation. My description of Spain might have absolutely inspired you, but it is quite possible that once there you would find you hated the place. Why? I don't know, because I don't know you as an individual. But suppose, for instance, that you are a very fervent Baptist. You'd have a dickens of a time worshipping in Spain. The state religion is Roman Catholic and it dominates the government like no other country in the world. You can't even marry a Spanish girl in your own church in Spain. You're a Roman Catholic, or else.

That, of course, is just one example. Perhaps you might dislike the fact that it is seldom that a movie is run in the local theatres in English; that there is no TV; that newspapers in English don't get to Spain until three days after they were printed. Perhaps you'll find that you don't like Spanish food—it's delicious, in my estimation, but many Americans like the food they're used to and refuse to learn any others.

I think the point is made. You might absolutely hate Spain. I don't think that you would, but it's possible.

Very well, if you are thinking in terms of Spain, then find out everything about it that you possibly can before heading in that direction. If at all possible, make a preliminary tourist trip to investigate the country before making your big move.

If you have decided to remain in the United States and retire in our own country, your task of investigation is simplified. You should be able to take a trip to the locality you have chosen.

Beyond this investigation, you should spend a considerable time reading further on retirement.

Frankly, I recommend living abroad under your circumstances. What you get for your money is often more than doubled.

GROUP No. 2. Let us say that you have a limited monthly income. It is possible in some places in the world, and I have presented examples in this book to live somewhat frugally on limited resources.

I don't recommend it.

Even though in such places as the Balearic Islands, it is possible to secure your food, clothing and shelter on a meager amount, you find yourself without reserves and the smallest emergency that comes up leaves you in a tight spot. You'll have to augment your income in order to lead a care-free life and that is what we want. The idea of retirement is to escape from the pressures of modern life.

So I suggest that you go through this book again and choose, not only the location in which you wish to retire, but also figure out where you yourself think you could swing.

Then, as recommended above for those persons with a larger income, investigate thoroughly everything you can find out about both the country and the business you are thinking of going into.

Make haste carefully in this matter of going into retirement. The fact that you are intelligent enough to be reading this book and investigating the possibilities of retiring while still young, is proof that you are also intelligent enough to progress toward your goal with proper precautions all along the line.

Any amount of regular income is priceless in retiring. Even though you may only have a small monthly income coming in, it's a great help and makes it that much the easier to find the full life you seek.

GROUP No. 3. I have seen both men and women, and even families, blow their tops, quit their jobs and jump down off the treadmill without a cent in their pockets. And make a go of it.

But I don't recommend it.

It's possible, but difficult. You can do it, but you'll have a hard row to hoe and particularly if you have dependents.

I strongly suggest that if you haven't any reserves at all, and no income, that you plan this out even more carefully than those preceding two groups. I don't mean by this that I am reneging on my promise to show you Retire Happily with Less Money, I'm merely charting a course for you to guarantee that you won't go on the rocks.

First of all, there's a good chance that you are currently in debt. Only a comparatively small percentage of working class families in the United States are free of debt.

I do not recommend that you attempt to go into retirement with the sword of debt dangling from a horsehair above your head.

Get rid of it.

By whatever means it takes, get rid of it.

If things are such that it will take a year for you to get free of your present debts, even by cutting every corner, then postpone retiring until you are free of them. You'd be hard put to retire, without a regular income, with a good deal of money owed.

However, I do make this suggestion all over again. Ask yourself, what it really is you want in life.

If those debts you have hanging over your head are for a large house, a larger one than you really want and need, I would suggest you think twice about saddling yourself for the next twenty or thirty years with those monthly payments. If it's a new model car, one of Detroit's fabulous monstrosities, I suggest you think twice about getting a smaller or cheaper one. Or even disposing of a car altogether. An astonishing number of Americans who have little need for an automobile saddle themselves with one. If your debts are for a whole flock of installment purchases ranging from TV sets to refrigerators, I would suggest you wipe them out as soon as possible, by whatever means is easiest.

If you really want to retire, you can do this. You can free yourself from debt and start fresh. Yes, you can. Remember that when we started this book we pointed out that you're going to have to get out of the keeping-up-with-the-Joneses state of mind. And that you must do.

I do not want to put over the impression here that my system of retirement means that for the rest of your life you aren't going to be able to enjoy some of the more expensive things of life. That's up to you and up to what you really want. If these things are what you really want you can acquire them—in time, and while still retired. But you're not going to be able to start off with no money at all, and no regular income, and support the usual pyramid of modern gadgets that the man on the treadmill has been taught he must have.

Okay. First of all, then, get free of debt by whatever means you must take.

Secondly, I suggest that you build yourself a suitable nest egg. You might have decided to go to, say, Greece, and take up making your own way. But obviously you'll need money for passage and at least a minimum to keep you until your project is under way. You'll probably also need at least a small amount of capital to get this project going.

I'm not denying that I know many people who have started retirement money making projects on nothing at all. In fact, I've done it myself in my time. But to the extent that you have a nest egg, no matter how small, you've parlayed up your chances.

How do you build a nest egg?

There are various methods, of course. It is possible that you can start your retirement project in your spare time, right now, while still working at whatever work-a-day position now supports you. As the project grows, and grow it will, if you've picked correctly, you'll get closer and closer to the point where you can quit the job.

Or possibly you can get a second job on the side, cut all expenses possible, even to the point of laying up your car, and save every cent you can get your hands on. If you are married and your wife is sympathetic to this retirement idea (or, if you're a woman, if your husband is) let her (or him) get a job, or a second job as well. Make a hobby of saving money. Eat cheaper food, move to a smaller apartment, and keep your entertainment costs to an absolute minimum. When you realize that your goal is retirement, a complete escape from this rat-race which has driven you to desperation, you'll find that a year's time devoted to building up a basic amount of capital with which to get started, can actually be fun.

Most Americans attempt to live-it-up far more than is necessary. If you've decided that retirement is your aim and pull every trick you can think of to acquire a starter, you can do it.

Once you have this, proceed much as I have suggested for those readers who have a small income. Select the American bargain paradise, or the foreign one, which appeals to you most and study up on it.

And then go to it!

Tens of thousands of your fellow Americans have retired, starting absolutely from scratch, and have made a wonderful, satisfying success of it.

Chapter 18: Strategies to be Wealthy

You cannot retire successfully unless you have an assured income or great confidence in securing an adequate income. I want to give you a little lesson in economics—not the kind of economics you might learn in schools or in colleges. In fact, I don't know of any schools and colleges that will teach you this kind of economics. But this is the kind of economics I live by, the kind of economics I have succeeded with. It may be cruel and heartless as many have informed me, but riches are not garnered by soft philosophies and kid gloves.

As a starter you must remember this—keep it in mind always lest you unwarily fall into the wrong hands. ALL WEALTH IS THE END PRODUCT OF LABOR. EVERYTHING THAT HAS VALUE IS VALUABLE BECAUSE OF HUMAN LABOR EMBODIED IN IT. All that is useful is not necessarily valuable. For example, water is our most useful product. Yet it is practically free because little labor is necessary to acquire it. On the other side not all things are valuable because labor may be embodied in them. You can go out and spend twenty days with a pen knife and a piece of timber to make a wagon wheel. A great amount of work has been expended but the labor embodied in all this has not been applied to create a socially desirable product. Hence the labor is worthless. ANOTHER POINT! ONLY EFFICIENTLY APPLIED LABOR CREATES NOTEWORTHY WEALTH. Which is to say that labor is expended unnecessarily unless the best and latest production techniques are utilized? Who would think of using lung power to blow bottles and glasses in these days when a machine, itself a magnificent example of embodied human labor of various and manifold types, can make hundreds of thousands of bottles and glasses during the same period of time.

NOTEWORTHY WEALTH is those products which command a price in the market place. In the long run all products exchange the one for the other at their value. Price is but the monetary reflection of this value, that is, embodied labor. At times price may be above or below the value of a product, depending upon the supply and the demand. But in the long run the price will revolve around a hard core—THE VALUE OF THE PRODUCT. AND LABOR CREATES ALL VALUES! Never be fooled or convinced otherwise on that score. Look again at the most useful thing in the world—water. It is practically free for the taking. Its value is nil. In the deserts it has value and market price—because it requires labor to acquire and bring it to that desert point where it is in demand—where it is needed and wanted. LET US LOOK NOW AT SOME OF OUR MOST VALUABLE COMMODITIES. Diamonds for example. A diamond cutter may spend days cutting just one diamond. It required quite an expenditure of labor in the first place to mine the diamond. A considerable amount of labor is expended in marketing the diamond. A diamond is tremendously valuable in the market place. Yet it is of less real use than a gallon of water. It is valuable because first it satisfies a human want and is, consequently, in demand as a prized possession. But its real value lies in the labor embodied in its manufacture and distribution. There are many stones that rival its beauty but few so valuable—BECAUSE THEY DO NOT REPRESENT ANYWHERE NEAR AS MUCH EMBODIED LABOR!

AGAIN MAY I ASK YOU TO REMEMBER THIS. LABOR IS THE SOURCE OF ALL VALUES! All products are regarded as commodities, bought and sold on the market place at various prices, depending upon the supply and demand. Some are expensive, some are said to be cheap. BUT LABOR IS INVARIABLY CHEAP. IT'S THE BIGGEST BARGAIN UNDER THE SUN! IT CAN ALWAYS BE BOUGHT RIGHT! I have bought and sold the labor of hundreds of people in my day! The price I paid was a stipend known by the kindly name of wage—or salary. What I paid was marketable for two to five times that much. That's a markup few finished products will ever stand. THAT IS A MARKUP THAT LABOR WILL ALMOST ALWAYS STAND. The product labor creates usually markets for many times its price, that is, what is paid for it in the form of wages. Perhaps you saw in my literature the mention of wage slavery. I meant that. Let me give you an example.

Back in the early part of the nineteenth century we had an institution in this country known as chattel slavery. Negroes were bought and sold in the market place. They were owned as property just as today we own horses, cattle or sheep. They were owned for only one purpose. For the extraction of wealth which their labor created. It was no secret. It was an open affair. A slave was a valuable piece of property. But a slave presented certain problems. He had to be kept in the peak of condition—otherwise he lost his use value and his market value. A sick slave had to be kept and nursed. He couldn't put out the work. If he became crippled it was like throwing money in the fire. He became worthless. The master had to feed and clothe him, shelter him and assure his fitness—just as today cattle and hogs are kept in sleek market condition.

But the Industrial Age reasoned this way. Why should I be Sam's keeper? Why go to all that expense? Pay him a little money instead; let him fend for himself. It's cheaper that way. If I need him he'll be there ready to give out for a stipend. If I don't need him I won't be burdened with him. If the market is slow I won't have to keep him in food, clothing and shelter just the same. I can turn him out. He'll be there waiting till I need him again. He doesn't have any place to go. I get what I want out of him just the same—his ability to labor. And the stipend I pay him is considerably less than the expense of maintaining him comes good or bad times. He's not a burdensome worry on me any longer. With this reasoning came about the institution known as the wages system—wage slavery, if you please. It was slavery in another form—a devious form that was not nearly so readily recognized. But slavery it was nevertheless and a form of slavery it remains.

Things are bad, economically, just now. I can place an ad today for help and tomorrow I can have hundreds of applicants knocking on my door, ready and eager to work for me, begging and pleading their consideration over that of competing applicants. Many will accept my terms, my offering wages. "Never mind what you got before. Why don't you go back there? Oh, they just laid you off. Well, if you want' work for me this is it. You don't want to starve do you? Well, I can hire plenty at this wage." And I got my prices all rigged in advance, of course.

WHAT I WANT TO GET ACROSS TO YOU IS THIS. YOU CAN DEAL IN THIS COMMODITY TOO! Labor is woefully ignorant. It knows not its value, it realizes little what wealth it creates, and knows little enough about its market price—wages. You can buy it and sell it wholesale. This is one important ingredient that created every great fortune today. Oh, of course, many acquired great wealth that was not dealing in this wonderful commodity, labor, directly. But they were dealing in the wealth that labor had created, or something that would be valuable only if labor were applied upon it. Again, remember that HUMAN LABOR is the cheapest commodity under the sun! Can you utilize it to your advantage? Can you direct its use in some marketable service or product whereby you reap a bountiful harvest?

I have employed workers as far back as I can remember, here and there, even back in Oklahoma in my teens. When I was a High School boy, it was the custom for a farmer to have the pecan trees thrashed on his place by someone else. It was a dangerous job to climb and thrash trees, especially if you were a farmer well along in years. Pecan harvesting was so hazardous that it was customary to gather the crop for 50% of the harvest. Indians were best suited for this kind of work and could best do it, but what decent Indian would think of work if he were drawing Indian relief? I made arrangements with several farmers in the river bottom areas to thrash their pecans. Some had groves of them, some had only a few trees. Thrashing begins after the first few frosts and lasts well into December, a period covering as much as two months. Some trees yield as much as two to three hundred pounds of pecans and these trees can be mammoth affairs to boot. With pecans at .15 a pound on the market at that time, I did very well. I climbed trees in the evenings after school and hired other school boys to help me. I had boys and girls gathering nuts from under the trees. On some Saturdays a crew of us managed to thrash five or six of these trees and come up with as much as eight hundred to one thousand pounds of pecans, half of which was mine. In those days wages were only $7.00 an hour for men or boys. I paid off my helpers and often managed to come out with $500 or more for a day's work. But tree skinning wasn't to my liking and for a few seasons pecans never bore because of adverse weather conditions during the spring season. I got the wanderlust too, even before I finished High

School. Otherwise, I imagine I would still be down there signing up every farmer with a contract to harvest and market his pecans. I had great ambitions about it at that time.

The point to grasp here is that I, by myself, could have done very little in the way of thrashing pecans and gathering pecans. If I had been working for someone else I might have received $7.00 an hour for my labor. But, as it was, I hired others to help me, paid them the 7.00 per hour and made a tremendous profit thereby.

In fact, I didn't even remunerate my labor until I had already marketed their product, the pecans. And this can be the case with you too! Why should you pay for labor before you have put much of its product on the market? I am presently an employer. I pay my employees weekly. And I am not paying them for the work they did this week. NO SIR! They are getting paid for the work they did for me—LAST WEEK!

A little capital can go a long way. Perhaps you have heard of the contraption known as the COTTON PICKER. They aren't the best machines in the world because they can't hold a torch to a man dragging a cotton sack down a row. That is, from their performance in the field. They leave fully a third of the cotton lying loose on the ground and the cotton gathered is full of leaves, bolls, stems and whatnot. The cotton lying on the ground after a cotton picker is usually picked up on the halves, by Mexicans in the West Texas district of whence I speak now.

A Cotton Picker will gather up to 25 bales of cotton a day with two operators. The best a boll puller can do by hand is around 1000 pounds if he really puts out. The average is around 500 pounds. It requires 2000 pounds of cotton in the boll to make a bale. Can you see the tremendous advantage a Cotton Picker with two operators that gathers up to 25 bales a day has over two boll pullers who between them can gather only 1/2 bale?

The acquisition of wealth is not exactly an easy task. If you have a penetrating mind you might turn up more situations than you can hope to cope with. This is my case. In fact, I sometimes find myself spread too thin on a project to project basis. At heart I am lazy and the comment has been made about me that I have worked harder getting out of work than if I had just went ahead and done the work in the first place. But my sort of laziness has developed an imagination that I am proud to brag about. And I can see opportunity in just about anything—perhaps from my varied background and experience—and perhaps because I try to look at it from the viewpoint of "How can I make something out of this and still be down on the creek fishing?" I have heard it said that it was the lazy man who was faced with work that invented a way of getting around it. I have a great love for the wealth and pleasures of this world. I don't intend to let work or duty stand in my way. As long as the commodity—LABOR—is around at such a bargain and is so ignorant why should I involve myself? I can live off the fruits of labor as long as I can utilize it efficiently and competently in the creation of a marketable product or service.

Do you imagine for one minute that the great industrial empires of this day were created by those who own them? If you do just how naive can you are? Is it not just possible that the half million workers whom a giant industrial corporation employs had something to do with the creation of the tremendous wealth the corporation holds title to? Did you know that many corporations have a net worth exceeding the net worth of all their employees combined by as much as 500%? The expression "He went out and made a fortune" isn't exactly true. "He so directed the activity of others that he made a fortune." Labor that works for a mere wage is much like the sheep that gives up its wool for a little food. It gives up just a whole lot more than it gets in return. It is really incredible that the great body of humanity permit themselves to be mulcted so pitifully by a mere handful who owns our industrial wealth. But that is the situation. And with the situation this way why can't you in your little way evolve a little system of your own for dealing in labor to your advantage?

Remember again! To acquire wealth you must somehow lay title to the product of the labor of another. You, yourself, by your own effort, cannot hope to create much wealth beyond your own comfortable needs. The legal way to lay claim to another's labor is to acquire his labor at a price which is considerably less, perhaps only a fraction, of its real market price. When you have mastered the situation to the point where you can employ one kind of labor to manage and corral another kind of labor, then you can free yourself of the whole process, go where you please, when you please, live as you please and enjoy life to its hilt. Others have done it from time immemorial and continue to do it. Why not you, too?

Chapter 19: Key Things to Remember

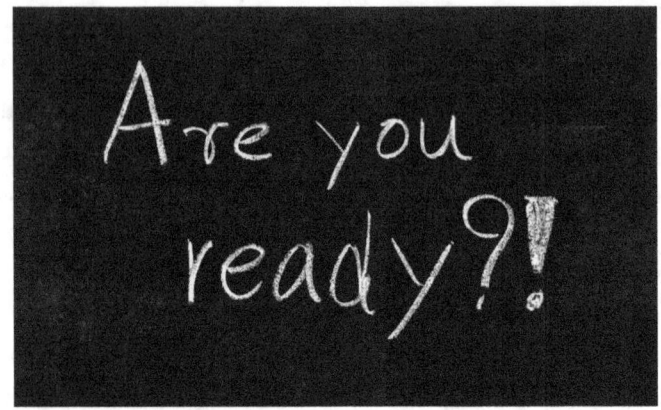

How to Use Your Imagination. Imagination is a dream searching for fulfillment. You will find it wise to dream. Dream magnificent dreams—the wildest dreams. Incorporate your ambitions and wants into these dreams. What would make you happiest in the whole world? Well dream about it. Picture this dream. Fix it in your mind. Now just how impossible is it? What would you have to do to make it come true? What can you do? What have you that will help you in the way of realizing this dream? What does it really take? Imagine yourself taking every step to realize your dream's fulfillment. Do any embryo plans begin to present themselves? Does any idea come to you that you can use to bring this about?

Dreams are the stuff ambition is made of. Dreams beget interests and pursuits. Dreams are the basic raw material for ideas, plans and, eventually, a course of action. Dreams are easy. They spring from desire. But putting dreams on the drawing boards—and thence to a material reality is beyond the average person. A thousand miles of dreams will draw them only a mile along the road. Better mileage any worthy dream deserves.

Don't be afraid of being labeled an idle dreamer. If you use your imagination enough sooner or later you'll give birth to a dream desirable enough and practical enough for you to undertake its realization. I subscribe to being a dreamer. During my younger years my dreams ran into fantasy. They were not practical by any stretch of the imagination. But of these impossible beginnings were laid the groundwork for mental projections of a more realizable nature. My tastes began to become definite and cultivated along certain lines. I began to find things I liked well enough to have in this world. My fantastic dreams gave way to the realization that every want we really have can be satisfied fully in this world we have in hand. I still, on occasion, dream on an astronomical basis.

But I manage to boil something little and something worthwhile out of them. Little inventions are the practical stuff of big dreams. Personally, I do not limit my dreams to this or that.

Whatever strikes my fancy or interest I delve into. How does a dream—or an imaginative project—like this sound to you. Let's try to create an engine that operates directly upon the heat of the air! I have heard a hundred persons say it was impossible for everyone who thought it was practical. But I have had no one to tell me why it couldn't be done. That is impossible too! If it can't be done there must be reasons why. If it can be done there must be reasons why. Can't you just imagine such a machine—a machine where fuel costs were no consideration? The heat of the air is ever renewed by the Sun. Why can't it be extracted or captured? We humans feel we utilize tremendous amounts of power but our power use is minuscule comparatively. I, personally, have had a lot of fun with this particular idea among others. It would be a great dream to have such tremendous energy that oceans of fresh water can be pumped to great deserts and be turned into Eden's of plenty. But in some of my encounters with unimaginative engineers I have come across arguments against it on the basis that it was perpetual motion, etc., etc. In fact, the impossibility of the idea was so stressed that I confess I made fools of some of them. What is not— is impossible. But many educated men cannot see this idea—when such is no longer just an idea. The heat pump is an embryonic beginning of just such a development.

The difference between great men of accomplishment and impractical fools is not as great as you might think. Dreams that are boiled down on practical premises can materialize. Dreams that are based falsely produce disappointment and despair.

Getting back to our subject in hand, that of retirement; put your dream power to work on it. Have you nerve enough to try to realize your dreams—just one good one? The steps you take to realizing your dream will not only net you happiness in their realization and fulfillment but in the engrossing activity along the pathways they lead you.

A negative way to approach the subject of ambitions and dreams is to take out of your life all that you DON'T LIKE! What are you dissatisfied with? What makes you unhappy? What misfits your tastes and comforts—your mental ease? What are you hopelessly hooked with? Are you not free? Why can't you chuck it all? Is your misery so important to the world? To you? Do you owe the world a miserable temperament? Must you reflect its ills in yourself? Do you feel you're going to live more than once—that you will have a second chance? It's about time you woke up! Happiness is worth going after—NOW!

The problem arises as to HOW. Here is where I have tried to help you. Courage is you lacking in? Will you listen to those who say it can't be done? Will you insist on being tied down? Can't you take a bold step and ACT? NOW? Start your dreams on the basis of WHAT YOU WANT TO GET AWAY FROM! When you start your dreams and pursue them consistently, plans for their fulfillment will evolve. Human nature has some "DO" in it and I think you have some "DO IT" in you, otherwise you wouldn't have bought this book.

Take my advice and dream, dream, dream. When you mentally traverse the road to the pinnacle of your dreams you will bring it down to the pathway of achievement.

WHY RETIRE YOUNG? I think I have stressed this throughout my book. Why waste your life? It's yours and you're going to live it only once. Why not get all the mileage you want out of it while you can? What this might mean in your particular case depends on your tastes and bent. But whatever it is, as long as they are worthwhile human motives you should not defer their realization until you can no longer enjoy them should you be able to. With advancing age we are able less and less to appreciate many of the physical activities of life through participation. What you can enjoy as an older person is far removed from what you can enjoy now. Don't dream of your old age in the terms of present wants. If you want something now—better try to enjoy it now. There is no reason in the world why you should not retire at 25 instead of 65, if, in so doing, you do not shirk your social obligations—or at least—prove a drag upon society. In my own opinion the world should be filled with happy fun-loving people. Don't permit your life to be so harsh that you are denied happiness now—and in your later years.

HOW TO CHOOSE THE RIGHT CLIMATE. I am not in the health field. But there are climates which are better from the standpoint of health, happiness and pursuits in which we find pleasure. As a general observation it is said that cold changeable climates make industrious people and warm climates make indolent pleasure loving people. Fortunately, because man can control his climate indoors wherever he may be, no longer need heat put a damper on our ambitions or industriousness, nor a cold climate prod us along the byways of dreariness. On the whole the right climate depends 'In what you seek. Health, sport, outdoor life or what do you want? As a retired person you are not necessarily tied down to a particular climate or locale. But if you want to settle down you should choose the one you like best and one that likes YOU. Keep in mind that the healthier areas of this country are in the South— Florida, Texas, Arizona, and other southerly states. Before you settle, travel a lot. It even pays to move around a bit. The people you settle among will be more of a consideration than the climate. And you will find all kinds of people somewhere in the great "retirement belt" of the Southerly states. In choosing your retirement area definitely considers the climate factor. It has a lot to do with human happiness.

WHAT? WORK IN RETIREMENT? Work need not be boring. I get a great pleasure out of writing. I can write effortlessly into the wee hours of the morning. Doing the work that you like is not work at all—it is activity that accomplishes and satisfies.

Idleness, especially for younger people, is the worst thing in the world. We have to have a sense of belonging in the world, a sense that we are contributing something to it, that we are "getting somewhere," that we are accomplishing something. This urge varies with the various parts of this country and with various parts of the world. You can lose your social consciousness altogether—if your associates in your area have also lost or never had such a social awareness.

Work while in retirement is healthful just as is exercise and recreation. But the work must be wholesome, interesting. You must be free to do the work or not to do it. It must not demand of you— in better words you are the master of the work; it does not own you. It can be no more than a work project or a hobby. It can or cannot be the source of your income, depending on your circumstances. If you must work and it is unpleasant, it may be little gain over your present circumstances.

By all means, if you retire, find some useful and soul satisfying activity to absorb your hours. Few people I know could really be happy while completely idle. For you, I would say, there are too many useful and soul satisfying pursuits to follow in this world while living in a retired or semi-retired state to let idleness bore you.

ALL right, that's it. You can do this thing. You can retire, starting right now, as of this minute. Before you know it, you are on your way to real life.

The treadmill, the rat-race, the carrot-on-the-stick chasing existence, the workaday world; all these you can forget. It's up to you.

Good luck.

MEET THE AUTHOR

Steven Young's goal is to encourage anyone at any stage of their life enjoy a life of financial wellness, both in this day, whatever it may hold, and in the future.

He has many years of experience of traveling abroad and enjoying life to its fullest wherever he calls home. Anyone can achieve financial freedom and cut their ties to the 9-5 daily grind that is full of stress and resentment. Open your mind to alternative ways of living and start planning how to make your retirement dreams happen.

Steven wasn't always the gypsy that he is today. As a young boy he learned the value of earning a dollar off of other people's labor. By following his instincts Steven has prospered as a business man and never followed the herd. Steven sought out a financial mentor, and began the journey of claiming control of his financial future.

Steven loves sharing picture and telling tales of faraway places that most people only dream. He does this to inspire people to start taking action towards achieving their own retirement dreams.

www.ingramcontent.com/pod-product-compliance
Lightning Source LLC
LaVergne TN
LVHW021943060526
838200LV00042B/1907